COMING AROUND

For Jesse, Haley, Grant, Nate, and Marin,
and for Marina, ever in the loving presence of
Presvytera Genovefa Nicolaou Newlin.

DAWN
COYOTE
PRESS

Dawn Coyote Press LLC

inquiries@dawncoyotepress.com

ISBN: 978-1-7360837-0-3 (print)
ISBN: 978-1-7360837-1-0 (ebook)

Ordering Information:
Special discounts are available on quantity purchases by corporations, associations, and others. For details, contact inquiries@tinaberger.com, www.tinaberger.com

CONTENTS

COMING AROUND

SURPRISES AND SURRENDER
on the path to
INSPIRATION

TINA BERGER

Introduction

I didn't write this book because I wanted to. I have wanted to write a book for years and never managed to do so. The truth is, this book came to me, and I somehow managed not to kill it. In fact, every time I attempted to impose my will upon its creation—whether by giving myself a deadline, trying to force it into a traditional structure, or simply reordering a sentence or two to conform more to the grammatical conventions I'd been taught—the energy and inspiration I had for the writing immediately evaporated.

So this book is here because I finally surrendered to it. I opened myself to receiving it, allowed it to speak its piece, listened as carefully and deeply as I could, and brought my best efforts to represent its messages as faithfully as possible. Over and over, I gave myself to writing down what came. And in time, I realized that this book was telling the stories that would eventually serve to explain its own creation. This book is the result of an inner collaboration—a divine balance between the feminine-receptive and masculine-assertive energies at once present and active in my own consciousness.

I didn't grow up thinking about things like divine balance. I went after life with arms wide open, not realizing there was anything missing until, as a young mother, I came face-to-face with the fact that something was seriously out of sync in my life. And it wasn't just circumstances from facing a divorce or issues at work. There was something profound that was missing in me: *I* was out of balance.

This book is partially my memoir. It tells certain stories of my life. Some of these stories seem fantastical and far-fetched, even to me, but they are real accounts of my ongoing life journey—my quest to remember and reclaim the parts of myself that I'd left behind in order to achieve academic and career success. As I tell these stories, I also offer descriptions of practices or experiments you might be inspired to try on your own journey.

I grew up traveling with a military family, so I know the world as my home. As a child, I moved joyfully and unselfconsciously in the spirit of the creative—every moment full of curiosity and potential. I loved music and singing. I wanted to be Elvis or Johnny Cash when I grew up, and I was pretty sure such things were possible. A kinetic force to be reckoned with, if I wasn't hanging upside down on the monkey bars, you might have found me riding my bike down the tallest hills in the neighborhood or playing dodgeball with the boys. It thrilled me to explore my physical limits, and—much to my mother's dismay—I broke a few bones along the way. But there was also a quiet side to my curiosity.

I was a voracious reader, fascinated by biographies and captivated by books that explained how things worked—from motorcycles to vaccines to electricity. I also liked a good Nancy Drew or Hardy Boys mystery, and two or three of these were often in my weekly library haul. I called myself an artist without hesitation. I sat for hours sketching horses, houses, and heroes, often gifting these creations to friends at school. I accepted these different expressions of myself without effort.

By the time I was 30, that young spiraling explorer felt a thousand miles away from who I'd become. I'd learned to make solid plans and execute them. I'd done well in school and was on the fast track to success with my corporate career. I wanted to "get there fast," wherever "there" was, and I tried hard to "do things right," to excel and achieve both personally and professionally. On top of all that, I had great friends and a supportive family. And yet, even though my life was progressing according to plan, I couldn't escape the nagging feeling that something was missing.

Then one day my life's path was diverted. I had no idea of either the destination or the nature of the work ahead. I didn't know how long it might take or even how I would begin it, but none of that mattered; my soul had already set things in motion. The genie was out of the bottle. The cat was out of the bag. Somewhere along the line—in my dauntless pursuit of excellence and success—I'd lost my inspiration.

So I set out to reclaim it.

The great Chinese philosopher Lao Tzu once said, "A journey of a thousand miles begins with a single step." In my case, it began with lots of self-help books and a series of experiments. The lessons I learned over the course of this journey moved and motivated me to make significant changes in my life: changes in how I parent and approach relationships, how I work and make decisions, and how I choose to spend my time.

This quest has taken me on thrilling adventures—both inner and outer—from exploring my most tender insecurities on my knees in the temple at Burning Man to being part of a joyous spiral of co-creation in Terrassa, Spain. And, ultimately, it's taken me to the writing of this book.

For me, sharing these stories with you is both an offering of tremendous love and a deep wish for the most compassionate and beautiful kinds of remembering and communion.

The Divine Balance: Referencing Masculine and Feminine

Throughout this book, I use the terms "masculine" and "feminine" in a way that may not be familiar. When I refer to the "masculine-assertive" and "feminine-receptive," I am not referring to biological sex, gender identity, gender roles, or gender expression. Instead, I am referring to a model much older, more stable, and more consistent in the human psyche. This model has shown up consistently through time, across cultures, and in spiritual traditions worldwide.

We may be most familiar with the symbol of the Tao, in which the masculine-assertive (yang) is depicted in harmonious balance with the feminine-receptive (yin). These models show us that humans can express masculine (assertive) and feminine (receptive) energies in any combination, regardless of biological sex (see table on page 195).

Psychoanalyst Carl Jung used the terms "anima" to refer to the feminine-receptive aspect of the psyche and "animus" to refer to the masculine-assertive. Because of the consistent ways in which these aspects of the psyche show up in our unconscious dream life, he referred to them as "archetypes." He associated the feminine with receptivity, intuition, interrelatedness, the emotions, and natural cycles. And he associated the masculine with directed action, such as doing or building, and with logic or rationality, individuality, and linearity.

CHAPTER 1

Spirit Vibrates at the Level of Amusement

When I asked about the psychic reading, the shop manager said, "Yes, Dawn can see you now." Delighted, I bookmarked her name in my mind: "Dawn." Of course—the sparky beginning of a good story. I didn't believe in psychics, but I felt a bump of curiosity and a cynical sort of amusement at the idea of taking a funny story back to my friends.

I was 31 years old and had just been promoted to lead the Houston region of a growing consultancy. A group of my friends and colleagues wanted to celebrate my promotion. Noticing that I was taking some strain as a newly single parent of a toddler, they'd pooled funds to send me on a solitary weekend retreat to San Francisco, even going so far as to arrange for my mom to watch my two-year-old while I was gone. On the flight there, I decided I was going to do everything as much in San Francisco style as I could. I'd visit Lawrence Ferlinghetti's City Lights bookstore, ride the trolley everywhere, visit Haight-Ashbury, take in an art show, and maybe even eat vegetarian.

This was how I came to be standing in a little New Age shop near Ghirardelli Square. I saw the sign from the other side of the street and made a beeline for the door: "Psychic Readings: 15 minutes for $25."

Surely this was one of the most San Francisco things one could do. It was just a quick gag for me, a new goofy adventure. I didn't come for advisement. I didn't believe I needed any.

When she came to get me for my reading, I felt a little disappointed. Dawn didn't exactly look or act the part of the psychic reader. No head wrap. No crystal ball. She sat down in an office chair and invited me to sit in the empty chair directly across from her. She asked me if I'd ever had a psychic reading, and I replied I hadn't. She told me that her method was to read energy, that she could see people's "auras."

Okay, I thought, why not? I felt confident in the way I saw the world. I kept my worldview flexible and open for a bit of mystery—though not enough for what was about to happen. Yes, I was very open-minded in the way that only self-assured, successful, and practical people can be. I wouldn't have necessarily argued *against* astrology, tarot, or meditation; I just assumed such things were a waste of time compared to, say, planning.

Dawn went on to set my expectations. She explained that while she did the reading, her eyelids would flutter and she might giggle from time to time. "Spirit," she told me, "vibrates at the level of amusement."

My interest piqued, I nodded my readiness and she began with a prayer for "a safe container" for the reading. Then almost immediately, with eyelids aflutter, she told me, "I see a tremendous amount of energy around your head…It's clear you have a very strong intellect. I have the impression of lots and lots of books, many of them related to religion and spirituality…"

I felt pleased with—and maybe a little too proud of—this beginning; I was also surprised that she had guessed so accurately at something so specific. For years I'd been poring over books on world religions, comparative theology, and ancient wisdom traditions. I'd always had an unquenchable thirst for learning about the ways in which people experience and define God.

She went on "…but even though you have read so many texts and accumulated so much knowledge of religion and spirituality, you don't actually practice any of the teachings you've learned in all of this study. You don't," she said, "know *the actual experience of spiritual connection.*"

My mind reeled and buzzed; I scrambled inside to get my bearings and take in what she was telling me. *Was she saying I wasn't doing it right?* I took pride in my critical thinking ability. I was known and appreciated among my friends and family for being logical and levelheaded. What did she mean by "the experience of spiritual connection?" Her voice interrupted my thoughts.

"You spend a lot of time in your 'astral,'" she explained, pointing to the space right above my head. "This means you're not fully embodying the physical experience of your life. You're holding most of your energy and consciousness *outside* of your body."

I felt that statement grab me hard by the shoulders.

"What I'm seeing in your energy," she said, "is that, as a child, you were extremely sensitive and emotional. And I'm seeing that this sensitivity worried the people around you…maybe your parents…because they didn't want to see you hurt. So at some point early in your life, you learned to disassociate from your strong feelings as a means of protection."

I swallowed hard, my mind tumbling, reaching to reconcile her words with my memories. She continued, "I can also see in your energy that you are completely shut down in your second chakra."

That statement threw me right back into my cynicism. I stifled a chuckle. I had no idea what my second chakra was, but it sounded like just the sort of New Age nonsense lifeline I needed in that moment. Perhaps sensing my skepticism, Dawn asked me if I wanted to know what it felt like to have energy move through my second chakra. My curiosity won out and I blurted, "Yes!"

So from her position across from and facing me, she lifted her hand and did a short series of waving and lifting motions—which sent a swooshing wave of intense energy and a roller-coaster sensation through my lower abdomen.

I started to bolt out of my chair. "Okay, okay!" I managed to gasp, holding my hands out in surrender, "Got it! Shut down in the second chakra!"

She gently explained that the system of the chakras is an eastern model that maps energy centers at specific locations along the spine. She told me that the second chakra is associated with the creative and sexual energies and also with the health of the sexual organs, so it was important that I find ways to reenergize that chakra. But by then, I was well over my capacity for taking in new information.

Soon after, Dawn closed the session, pressed a button on the tape recorder I'd forgotten about, and handed me a cassette of the reading. I paid the woman at the front desk, trundled numbly out of the shop, and shuffled two miles back to my hotel in the misting chill of the San Francisco air.

The accuracy of the reading itself was enough to have blown my mind, but this woman had "moved energy through my second chakra" *with a few waves of her hand.* And I felt that. Physically. In my body.

From Sleeve to Shelf: Forgetting Feeling

"There's no reason to cry," my dad offered, looking down into my crumpled nine-year-old face. "Think about it. She was very old and she was hurting and had been very sick. She wouldn't want you to be sad."

I believed my father, so I anchored to his face and followed his instructions: I thought about it. Almost immediately, I felt an emotional distancing, a subtle psychic shift, a stepping away from the gape in my heart. From this place, I felt strangely calm and comfortable with my grandmother's passing, somehow no longer feeling the losses of my sensory and emotional connections to her, the sound of her laughter, the smell of her apron, the special way she made my grits and eggs.

I remember, even then, being a little surprised at how easy this shift was for me to make. Looking back on it now, I feel I must have been naturally wired for that flexibility.

All I needed to do to relieve myself from feeling the loss of this grandmother who cherished me so was to push my awareness up out of my body and into my thinking mind. I say I must have been wired for it because I can't recall a time when I wasn't able to take a different perspective.

I remember, even as a much smaller child, running scenarios through my mind to imagine how a friend would react to the gift of one of my drawings or how my father would react to a passage in a book I was reading or how my mother would respond to a certain soulful song.

I remember once piling a little apple-sized mound of grassy dirt on the otherwise flat and manicured lawn in the park and watching from a distance to see how far out of their original trajectory people would walk in order to step on the little outlier of a grass mound.

So while I was a sensitive kid, I was also curious about people, what they thought, and how they responded to situations. This curiosity may have primed me for the flexibility in my perspective, or it may have worked the other way around.

The same evening that we talked about my grandmother's passing, my father drove me to the junior high gymnasium and gathered my Little Dribblers team, which he coached. He put his hand on my shoulder and encouraged me to have fun playing my basketball game.

Clearly an expert at the same kind of emotional dissociation he had suggested to me, on the day of his mother's passing, my dad could find no reason why we shouldn't just keep doing the things we had on the schedule.

As a child, I saw this kind of behavior as evidence that my dad was exceedingly strong and balanced. No matter what happened, I thought, he kept his cool, considered the options, and got on with the business at hand without being distracted by his emotions. Over time, I came to understand my dad's perspective this way— emotion was wasted energy. Logic, intellect, and action were the higher and more mature ways of experiencing and processing life's events.

I admired my father's calm in the storm and patterned myself after him in this way; I scored a few points that night, and in time, I developed my own reputation as a calm and levelheaded person who couldn't easily be thrown off her game.

My interactions with my mother reinforced some of these same messages in different ways. As the granddaughter of sharecroppers and the daughter of domestic servants, my mom knew hard work as a fundamental matter of survival. Sitting around indulging in one's thoughts or feelings just wasn't done; when she was growing up, there was no time or patience for such things. The potatoes needed digging, the clothes needed washing, the bread needed baking, and the younger siblings needed tending.

She brought that same approach with her when she immigrated to the US from her homeland of Cyprus. When my brother and I were little, she stayed busy cooking, cleaning, and caring for our family and home. Once we got a little older, she began working full time, often in jobs that were nontraditional for women. When I turned 12, my mom began training to be an electrician. Everywhere my mother worked, her coworkers and supervisors sang her praises. In every job she ever had, Mom was known for going above and beyond what was expected. I can't recall ever seeing her enjoying a relaxing bath or lounging on the couch. Seldom would she watch a 30-minute television show without also folding and sorting a basket of clean laundry.

I admired my mother's work ethic and patterned myself after her in this way, landing my first job at 14. I remember conversations with her about the importance of working hard. "If there are no customers in the store," she told me, "and you don't know what to do next, you make sure you go to your boss and ask him what other work he needs done. Don't waste his money standing around."

My first job was scooping ice cream at Baskin Robbins, and to my mother's great pride I was promptly recognized for my excellence in the nightly task of floor mopping (and not standing around).

While I knew that she went through hard times emotionally, my mom did her best to keep those things to herself, just as she was taught. As an immigrant, she had developed the useful habit of noticing how good she had it compared to so many others in the world with much bigger problems. After all, she'd left her small island to come to the US not long before Cyprus became embroiled in a violent conflict; some of my mother's friends and relatives disappeared, never to be seen again.

The abundant opportunities and enduring peace in this country were never things she took for granted. Through her, I learned not to dwell on unpleasant things, especially unpleasant things that couldn't be changed.

Yet Mom is highly empathic herself; I noticed early on that it pained her to see me hurting. She never communicated this to me directly, but I could feel her profound wish for me to be happy.

While unintentional, this pattern further reinforced my understanding that the best approach to painful or difficult emotions was to disconnect from them. Sometime before I turned 10, I developed a specific strategy for handling my sadness, anger, or hurt feelings that involved going directly to bed and willing myself to sleep, no matter the time of day. I found it much easier to keep my feelings to myself that way, and I was typically able to forget and release them after a nap.

The upside of these dynamics with my mother was that they also established in me a habit of remaining focused on the positive and always remembering my good fortune. Again, this way of relating to and moving in the world, of seeing my life as abundant with possibility, came easily for me as a child.

I do recall feeling sad at times, but I always kept an underlying optimism, an expectation that those feelings would pass, and an understanding that I was immensely lucky to be alive.

As a child, I also took great joy in moving my physical body. I would run and race until my face was red and my hair was drenched with sweat. I loved climbing trees, riding my bike, and spinning on the tire swing. I also loved to exercise my mind. I relished biographies and redemption stories of all kinds. I never tired of reading books and imagining all sorts of possibilities for my life. Would I be a doctor? An inventor? An artist? An Olympian?

Partly because of my own predisposition and partly because of my early training and reinforcement, I learned to lean out of my emotions and into my intellect. I learned to value action over stillness and presence. I learned to value goal-focused movement over wandering or spontaneity. In short, my expression tended to be overbalanced to the masculine-expressive aspect of my personality, my "yang."

Practically, this approach turned out to be quite handy: a blueprint for success in a culture and systems that consistently reward this way of expressing. I learned to "achieve."

In high school, I played sports and did well academically. Summers, I held full-time jobs. I was not a typical teenager. I became interested in basic carpentry and built my own bookshelves, collected a set of tools and tuned up my own car, and developed sufficient culinary skills to prepare a respectable range of meals.

During my senior year, I effectively checked out of the high school experience to work half days at a local hospital as part of a vocational program. At ages 16 and 17, I was transporting medicated patients back and forth to surgery, informing loved ones of a patient's post-op status, occasionally assisting surgical nurses by holding a limb during a surgical procedure, and cleaning operating rooms.

Unfortunately, the trade-off for all that doing and practicality was my social life. I had a small group of friends that I did things with, but I never really engaged with them beyond the superficial level. I didn't even know that engaging beyond the superficial level was a possibility. I was already living mostly in my head by then, so I didn't understand the point of dating in high school. I didn't know myself emotionally or sexually. My "logical" thinking about high school romances went something like, "Why are they pretending they are in love or that this dating thing matters in high school?" When the occasional guy did show interest in me (and the few that did were kind and lovely), I panicked and found a hundred ways to avoid him. This strategy helped me snuff out any burgeoning "feelings."

In my quiet moments, I felt confused and haunted by a vague sense of sadness. Looking back now, I see my teenage years were immensely lonely.

Fortunately, through my high school years, we lived near my mother's family. My self-image was buoyed by the loving presence of my aunts, uncles, and younger cousins who seemed not to notice or mind my social ineptitude.

As I started college, I had a good bit of catching up to do, socially. I didn't know how to initiate relationships. I often didn't know what my feelings were, much less how to share them. I didn't even know how to find the right cadence of communication to use with new friends. I got excited about a new acquaintance and overly focused on making plans with her or him. I tried to show my affection to friends by giving them something, a favorite record, a mixtape, or a charm from my small collection.

Sometimes I teased too hard, and I tended toward the sarcastic, which also pushed people away. The truth was, I had no real practice in establishing intimacy, recognizing social signals, or managing healthy boundaries.

Best Laid Plans

As it turned out, my love relationships became opportunities for me to learn more about the feminine-receptive—yin—aspect of myself. In his writings, the famous psychoanalyst Carl Jung refers to this feminine-receptive archetype as the *anima* and associates it with receptivity, intuition, interrelatedness, the emotions, and natural cycles.

At 21, I married for the first time—a marriage that serves mainly as a point of contrast for the lessons ahead. Neither Bill nor I had much going on in the realm of the feminine-receptive expression. We each had goals and plans for our lives, and we were focused on taking the most direct action to achieve them. In other words, we were much more aware of the *yang*, or masculine-assertive aspects of ourselves, and we amplified that kind of action-oriented energy in each other. It looked pretty good from the outside, and we managed to make it work well enough for a while.

We met at Baylor University where we were both on ROTC scholarships. I ended up joining ROTC because they had the shortest and fastest-moving line at freshman registration. As the first in my family to attend college, I had no idea what I was doing. When I arrived at the front of the line and began to select my courses, they offered me a military scholarship and I took it.

I'd never had any interest in being in the military, but I knew how to compete. I ended up being among the highest-ranking freshmen and sophomores in the organization before I left it.

Bill, on the other hand, took an ROTC scholarship because he had military aspirations. His dad was a fighter pilot, and Bill intended to follow the same path until a few bouts of asthma disqualified him. It was a joke between us that I always outranked him.

I called him Joe Scholarship because I thought he went a little overboard with the "military bearing." He took it all very seriously, devoting time to shining his shoes, practicing his briefing presentations,, and showcasing a snappy salute. He was a good sport about my teasing and, eventually, began bringing me flowers he had picked.

Why not date him, I wondered? He was a good guy. He was more structured, conservative, and traditional than I was, but that was what I had grown up with. It was familiar, and I appreciated the intellectual challenge of a good debate. We had compatible aspirations and we had some goofy good times together. That's how my inner dialogue ran at the time.

All in all, Bill was a caring person with a good moral compass, and we had an easy banter together. He was smart and ambitious and his goals were clear. He aspired to start up a business in the then still-emerging field of personal computing. He knew he wanted two children, a dog, a house, and a certain amount of money in savings. He also had developed a useful range of life skills from his experiences prior to college.

It seemed to me we were well matched, and at the time we were. We were both ambitious and driven with clear goals and solid plans for getting there.

We graduated from college and landed good jobs in the corporate world. We bought and furnished a lovely first home in the suburbs and began to save money for the future. While I felt tremendous affection for Bill and I loved him to the extent I was able to know love at that point in my development, the decision to get married was, for me, primarily a rational one.

I thought that's how such decisions were supposed to be made: Find someone you care for and with whom you can develop shared goals, get married, and get to work on planning for and achieving those goals together. Looking back, I see my decision to be with Bill was more intellectual than emotional. We both had so much to learn.

The weaknesses in our union became more evident and painful over time and were rendered in high relief after we adopted a dog. Being a practical person, I didn't really want a dog. I wasn't trying to sign on for more responsibility. But Bill had a plan for his life and that plan included a dog.

It's not a natural trait of any dog to be either (a) linear or (b) rational, but our dog, Franklin, excelled in the opposite direction and began, quite literally, to eat our house. The chaos and disruption this wild, sweet Aussie shepherd brought into our lives was overwhelming and unmanageable.

Franklin didn't conform to our vision for his life as a well-behaved dog, and that confounded us. He required a level of attention, care, and activity that we hadn't accounted for. We were busy trying to build careers, plan for a family, and take on the responsibilities of managing a household. We had neither the skills, the patience, nor the open hearts needed to nurture and train this puppy, and I can say without hesitation we failed him mightily.

We kept Franklin, but he was a constant source of contention and frustration. We had no real framework for how to deal with the situation; it was the perfect example of what was not working in our marriage. Franklin stayed wild. He dug up the yard over and over. He destroyed countless shade structures and toys.

Animals have a way of showing us our shortcomings with unmatched clarity. Franklin had a gift. He taught me the basis of one of the very few universal truths I have come to know: "If you have a problem with an animal, it's your problem." It was our problem. Neither Bill nor I ever figured out how to help Franklin burn off energy in a more constructive way, and so it went on.

Despite our failure to align on the best ways to care for Franklin the Australian shepherd, we somehow felt certain we could be strong parents. And, anyway, parenting was part of our plan. And so, at 29, we were over the moon to become first-time parents to our son, Jesse.

I viewed mothering as a new aspect of life that, while obviously a blessing, also brought with it a whole new set of "dos," things that must be done, that must be added to the large and growing list of daily actions that I felt were central to my worth and value.

Jesse emanated a radiance from day one. He often seemed like an old spirit trapped in a baby's body. He was bored rapidly with mobiles and rattles and other baby activities and became easily frustrated if he wasn't promptly assisted in his quest for new experiences. He insisted we carry him with his eyes facing forward.

I felt confused by my lack of pleasure in being a mom in comparison to what I expected and was certain I observed in others. I strove to do mothering right, to read to him enough, to make sure his clothes were clean and ironed, to engage him in stimulating activities, and to make sure he was bathed and his teeth brushed.

All of these things were added to my existing "to-do" list, which was already fairly daunting: grocery shopping, cooking, cleaning, laundry, exercising, and entertaining our friends and families.

This was how I thought life was supposed to be. I spent most of my time and energy in action mode, removed from knowing myself in a state of relaxation, often unaware of my own emotions. My focus on managing the plans and activities of caretaking left me unable to find time to be still and receptive. I can't remember much relaxed time spent holding, playing with, and being spontaneous with my child without feeling like I was falling behind on the things I needed to be doing.

As a new mother, I also experienced a pretty serious bout of postpartum blues, which I had no means for contextualizing or explaining given my "get 'er done" worldview. And neither did Bill.

Somehow, I wasn't experiencing any overwhelming joy or sense of fun. In the early '90s, the public conversation about postpartum depression had not yet begun, and we didn't have a robust internet to turn to for answers. I felt deep shame and confusion that I was not able to rise consistently above these feelings of sadness during what should have been one of the happiest times of my life.

As a side effect, these feelings cracked open within me a door to deeper emotional inquiry. I wanted to understand. I wanted to talk and explore and examine what was happening inside me. I wanted to figure it out. This shift in me created new challenges for Bill and me as a couple.

As I began to grapple with bigger questions about my innermost workings, I sensed that Bill longed for the simpler, more predictable relationship he'd signed up for. The distance between us grew, and we divorced before Jesse turned two.

We'd managed to hold the marriage together for eight years. But in the end, we were unable adequately to take each other in, to listen and collaborate well, to hold each other's hearts with sufficient compassion, and to develop enough emotional intimacy and trust to get through the rough parts of our life together—all of which, incidentally, are expressions of the feminine-receptive aspect.

A Certain Success

Much has been said about the "patriarchy," and the inherent sexism or suppression of the feminine that's often spoken of as if there is an ongoing intentional and aggressive silencing and suppression underway.

While I wouldn't begin to suggest that such a thing doesn't happen and isn't a very real part of our cultural history, my experience is that the patterns of suppression run well beneath the current level of public intention and consciousness. The bias in favor of the masculine-assertive expression and in opposition to the feminine-receptive expression is "baked in" to our systems, so there is a sort of widespread collective blindness to it.

The ethos of the American Dream—the belief that success and upward mobility are equally available to anyone and everyone willing to work hard—is still strong in our culture.[1]

I attribute my own success in corporate America to the work ethic, levelheadedness, and drive toward individual achievement that I learned from growing up in a culture that specifically affirms and recognizes these things: a culture that values and rewards those who express the masculine-assertive energies.

We generate success to the extent that we can conform to and match the preferences of our prevailing systems. For me, that has meant learning to lead with the masculine-assertive.

I learned to speak up and get my ideas into the room, to ensure those ideas are logical and rationally presented, to deliver my work according to plan and ahead of schedule, and to make my individual work and contributions visible. Initially, this approach was not so much a conscious choice for me. I approached my work this way because it's how I had learned to generate opportunities and success for myself. I simply believed it was the right way. After all, what value could possibly be gained by the alternative? I certainly wasn't going to wallow in my feelings, waste my time sitting in parks, and wait for good things to happen to me.

Unless we lean our expression toward the masculine-assertive and conform to the values that underpin our cultural and eco-

---

1 Mohamed Younis, "Most Americans See American Dream as Achievable," Gallup, November 23, 2020, https://news.gallup.com/poll/260741/americans-american-dream-achievable.aspx.

nomic systems, it is nearly impossible for us to generate success in those systems. Once again, I'm not referring to biological sex or gender identity, I'm referring to the masculine energies such as unwavering rationality, directed action, and assertiveness.

For example, men who lead with the *yin* aspects of relatedness, receptivity, and emotional sensitivity over logic have as much difficulty succeeding in our systems as women who express those same characteristics. And women like me, who learn to express the masculine aspects of assertiveness, rationality, competitiveness, and goal orientation often have no trouble generating economic and professional success in those same systems.

Consider the common descriptions of women who have risen to leadership in our government and major corporations. Hillary Clinton, for instance, is known for her drive, her accomplishments, and her ability to maintain her calm and rationality in a storm. I have no idea whether she possesses the flexibility to shift the balance of her expression toward the feminine-receptive to adapt to different contexts, but certainly people don't perceive her in that way. She has learned well to deemphasize her *yin* expression in the public, political forum.

CHAPTER 2

Lessons Not Lost on Me

Healing by Heart

She patted the couch with a gentle, comforting authority most often wielded by mothers and nurses. "Lie down here," Shannon directed. Shannon was my first female love and partner. Deeply empathic, Shannon's gifts as an intuitive healer astonished me.

My right temple was throbbing with the beginnings of a migraine. It was a familiar sensation, a pattern that had been plaguing me on and off for years. I knew how it went from here.

In very short order, I would be writhing in my bed in the dark with my head on a heating pad, sick to my stomach from the searing pain and ineffective migraine medicines. It would go this way for many hours before the pain relented. The episode would be followed by something like a hangover, forcing me to take it slow, move deliberately, and eat bland foods for another half a day.

As I lay flat on my back on the couch, Shannon placed one of her hands on my forehead and the other on the top of my head. As she did so, I felt an immediate sense of relief, a noticeable dulling of the pain.

Surprised, I opened my eyes. Shannon's own eyes were closed, her head tilted slightly to one side, her facial expression appearing as if she were listening intently to a whisper. Without opening her eyes, she lifted the hand that was resting at the top of my head and repositioned it so that it was about an inch away, leaving a small space between her hand and my head. She held it there, and after a few moments I sensed a disruption in the familiar pain progression that normally characterized my migraines. I could actually feel the interplay of the energy between the top of my head and her hand just above it. Whatever Shannon was doing somehow kept the migraine from intensifying.

After about 10 minutes, she lifted the hand positioned just above the top of my head and held it away from herself and me, intermittently flicking it as if she were shaking water off. She did this a few times before replacing her hand and repeating the process twice more. Then she stepped away, allowing me to sleep, my pain gone. This was the first of many times she would resolve my migraines.

Shannon had the ability to sense pain and illness in people and often to provide some relief from their suffering. On the receiving end, this combination felt nurturing, comforting, and, at times, very maternal. For much of the time we were together, friends and acquaintances in physical and emotional pain sought her for her comforting presence. She even served as a doula for women in labor, nurturing and encouraging mothers-to-be through the process of childbirth.

Shannon and I had met while working as technical writers on the same assignment. She was whip smart and had traveled the world. We had similar senses of humor and shared a lot of laughs while working long hours in client offices, meeting hard deadlines. Our friendship developed first, and over time the relationship grew more intimate after my divorce. We lived together for around six years, from the time Jesse was a toddler until he was 10.

I recognized the power and beauty of Shannon's intuitive gifts, and there was a part of me that was drawn to understand more deeply the nature of this way of being and relating. Through the lessons of this relationship, I began to feel more awake and open to the possibilities and the value of moving differently in the world.

There was a way in which I sensed Shannon never completely relaxed in our relationship. I was deeply in love with her, but I sensed in her a kind of vigilance. Years into our time as a couple, her preference was to keep our relationship under the radar and unacknowledged even to friends and family. We maintained separate bedrooms and separate accounts; it was an open secret among those in our circle, but we mostly didn't speak of ourselves as a couple. Some of this likely had to do with the fact that same-sex relationships were still not widely accepted or affirmed at that time.

Also, there was me. I was still learning how to be in relationship. I demonstrated love by taking care of tangible things like the laundry and the dishes. At times, my communication could still feel too pointed and judgmental, and I hadn't even begun to learn the art of emotional nurturing. I wasn't able to hold space for my own emotional expression, so how could I possibly create space for someone else who might need emotional support? These deficiencies were giant blind spots for me at the time.

Looking back, I still don't fully understand the challenges in our relationship dynamics. But I do wonder if there's something consistent in the relationship challenges between those who more naturally express the feminine-receptive and those—more like me—with an expression overbalanced to the masculine-assertive.

Would my embodiment and expression of the same bias found in our broad cultural and economic systems feel unsafe to someone who most naturally expresses the feminine?

Was Shannon picking up on and responding to my unexamined rejection of those feminine-receptive aspects, aspects which she most natively expressed?

I studied her intently for the years we lived together: The way she listened without interrupting, the way she intuited and empathized with the feelings of others, the way she preferred to take her time with decisions, mulling alternatives. In a way, this relationship marked the beginning of a pattern for me. I didn't realize it at the time, but in retrospect I can see clearly that I established and cultivated relationships partly as a means for being with and learning about the feminine-receptive expression.

I suppose it could be seen as a kind of unconscious bargaining. I traded my gifts of efficiency, practicality, logic, and predictability for the opportunity to engage, observe, and learn from the feminine.

Here Comes One

New lessons came from the relationship I developed with my second female partner, Kimberley. We met at a business conference. She was working in sales for a marketing company, and I went to her exhibit space to learn more about the services her company provided. We clicked when she came to make a sales presentation for the small company I was working for.

She had an amazing talent for marketing and communications and a funny "Lucille Ball" kind of shtick that I found hilarious. I thought she would make a great friend. I certainly wasn't looking for anything more. She was straight and married with two kids, and I was still in a relationship with Shannon, so I didn't perceive the attraction immediately. But one afternoon I met Kimberley for coffee, and she began earnestly to express her feelings and her desire to explore a romantic relationship with me. I knew I was in trouble and called my therapist on the way home.

I had never been taken in so completely and pursued so earnestly or passionately, and that experience really connected for me; it woke me up to the powerful realization that I needed something more in an intimate relationship than what had been possible in my partnership with Shannon. While Shannon and I were (and still are) great friends, we were not great romantic partners. And while I wasn't optimistic that a relationship with Kimberley was in the cards, I couldn't unknow what that connection showed me. I wanted to be wanted.

The next few years were both excruciating and thrilling as Kimberley and I dealt with the pain of ending long-term relationships and explored the possibilities for a life together. Expectations be damned, with a lot of grace from our exes and kids and not a small amount of support from professionals, we came through it all with our relationship still intact.

Throughout our 14 years as intimate partners, I found Kimberley's emotional range fascinating in its breadth and vastness. In the early stages or our relationship, her emotions could seem uncontained, often passionately and sometimes aggressively expressed. I was dumbfounded to find that there were times when she didn't know what had prompted the extreme expressions of anger or grief that arose in her. And she could be equally extreme in her expressions of compassion, love, and joy. She just felt what she felt and seemed to have no choice but to let the feelings out in their rawest form.

Kimberley was the first to introduce me to the idea of "feeling a room." When she walked into a room full of people, Kim had immediate and strong intuitions about how each person was doing emotionally. She could also sense the collective energy of the room and identify the sources of any discord or disharmony before even hearing a single word spoken.

I found this talent both mystifying and useful. Occasionally, she would take it on as an enjoyable personal challenge to interact with those in the room whom she sensed were hurting or most unhappy. I would watch in awe and delight as her playful interactions with those individuals shifted the feeling of a gathering into lightness.

During our time together, I came to recognize, deeply appreciate, and even depend on the significance of this gift of feeling.

I also recall being surprised and to be honest, at times, a little judgmental of the degree to which Kimberley could be emotionally impacted by a news story. A tragedy on the other side of the world could take her into a depressive funk for days. Over the course of our years together, however, I began to see and respect the truth of the sadness she would feel. I began to recognize the importance of attending to the deep wisdom of the sensitives, like Kimberley, living in our communities. These are the people who feel intensely their connection with others on the planet, the people who are able to share others' feelings of grief and loss during a heartbreak. In this sensitivity, Kimberley reflects the aspect of the feminine-receptive expression that knows, physically and psychically, our collective interdependence, the embodied truth of the statement, "When one hurts, we all hurt."

Even though I admired Kimberley's gifts, I confess in the early stages of our relationship I generally considered myself to be more advanced in my emotional and spiritual development. It makes me wince, now. I'd learned well by then how to spare myself and others the impact of my emotions.

For years, I imagined my way of remaining calm and cool to reflect the more evolved way of being. By contrast, Kim suffered with bouts of extreme anxiety and mood swings. Certainly, I projected the more stable, rational, and functional image. From the pedestal I'd built myself, I occasionally suggested she might try certain awareness practices to free herself (and me) from the tyranny of her unchecked emotions.

I loved her deeply and without reservation, but it is clear to me now how my behavior and my attitude could be at times demeaning in more and less subtle ways. In those feelings of superiority, I had the tacit support of our entire culture behind me, a culture that values my way of suppressing, intellectualizing, and controlling emotionality and getting on with the business at hand.

But it was through my relationship with Kimberley that I began to learn to nurture others and to hold emotional space. When she wasn't beset by anxiety, she was remarkably gifted at taking care of people who were physically or emotionally hurting, including me. She had a sense for when to be quiet, when to speak, what to say, what to bring, and how to create a loving space for people in such a way that they could receive comfort.

Even strangers could feel that receptive capacity in her. She was regularly approached in stores or public places by people who were sure they knew her. It happened so frequently that it became a joke between us. We would see a person approaching her, and one of us would whisper, "Here comes one...."

On one occasion, while we were out shopping together a woman approached Kimberley and asked her a question about the picnic baskets she was comparing. Almost immediately after Kimberley answered, the woman revealed she'd been recently diagnosed with cancer. I watched as Kimberley turned to face her, hold her hands, and take in her entire story. After about 20 minutes, with tears in her eyes, the woman thanked Kim profusely. She said she hadn't told anyone else about her illness and didn't know what it was about Kimberley that made her blurt it all out.

In the earliest years of our relationship, it seemed I had no natural instinct or gift for emotional presence or caretaking. My caretaking was all in the realm of "doing." During the years we were together, Kimberley and I co-parented my son, Jesse, and Kim's two children by her previous marriage, Haley and Grant. Although we shared parenting duties, my duties typically fell more in the realm of the practical and Kimberley's more in the realm of the emotional.

When one of our kids or Kimberley was ill or hurting, I filled the prescriptions, shopped for the groceries, kept the bathrooms clean, picked up the slack with childcare, and made healthy dinners. And I was exceedingly proud of myself in all this doing.

Kimberley eventually expressed some frustration with the lack of tenderness and empathy in my approach, and it hurt my feelings. In a very real way, I didn't know what she was talking about.

When she was ill, I was quite happy to bring her a cup of tea and sit with her for a few minutes if she asked. And I was very affectionate, generally. But nurturing, I came to understand, was altogether a different thing from affection; it's an attentive quality of receiving that allows you to feel into the needs of another and to create and hold a loving and comforting container for someone who's suffering. Over time, I learned to drop more into my own sensitivity, to understand and feel the difference, and to provide a more emotionally nurturing kind of care to those in my midst.

I stretched and developed more in my years with Kimberley than in all my previous years of life combined. Ours was an often funny, sometimes challenging, and always transformational relationship.

We raised amazing kids, went on wild adventures, took ridiculous gambles, and conducted big life experiments together.

One of our wildest adventures was embarking together on a wilderness rites of passage experience in Death Valley. I'd learned about this program while taking classes in ecopsychology at Naropa University. This experience involved gathering with a group of 12 in the desert. For the first four days, our guides shared teachings designed to prepare us to spend the next four days alone in the wilderness holding a clear intention for how we wished to embrace our next stage of life. During those four days, we would see no one, fast from food, and take in only water. At the end of our solo time, we would return to the group, and each person in turn would share the story of their experience with the group and the guides.

I described the program to Kimberley and told her it was something I wanted to do. Even though she wasn't much into roughing it, she surprised me with her immediate enthusiasm to sign up. But, then again, that was Kimberley's way: "Leap first. Ask questions on the way down."

She endeared herself to all the seasoned campers in our group, playing up her lack of preparation and regaling them with jokes and stories before asking to borrow any extra socks and warm pants, which indeed she needed for her time alone on the land.

After we completed the four-day fast and returned to reunite with each other and the group for a brief breakfast, we were given the afternoon to rest and recover before dinner. While we agreed the experience had been powerful, we also agreed we were tired of sleeping outside. We booked ourselves into one of the nicer resort hotels in the park and after a blissfully hot shower collapsed into the bed for a nap.

I'd drifted out of the fog of sleep when I heard Kimberley whisper, "I've had an intensely vivid dream."

I turned to face her and she continued, "I was visited by my people, my Irish ancestors. Oh, they were lovely and gentle, but they gave me a good talkin' to."

I realized suddenly, as she was relating the story of this dream to me, she was speaking in a smooth and subtle Irish brogue. I had by this point known Kimberley for 10 years, and in this moment I knew two things: she was not able intentionally to put on an Irish brogue accent (…if she were, I've not a single doubt she'd have been doing it all the time!) and she was not aware she was doing so in this conversation.

I managed not to interrupt or look amazed as she continued, "They said to me, 'Lass, ye'r missin' the point of yehr heritage. Ye only tell the stories of yehr people as drunks and horse thieves and fighters, but there's so much more to us…so much more! We are the source of yehr sensitivity, yehr ability to see the people and understand what they're feelin' and teh bring them some comfort. Yehr Irish people, we're storytellers and poets…we're the entertainers at the center of the crowd, singin' the songs, delightin' the people, and helpin' 'em forget their troubles!'"

I was rapt and speechless at this point; afraid that any interruption might derail the magic of the moment, so I actively managed my reactions.

She went on, "They told me if I only ever saw the bad things in my ancestors, if I only ever saw them as scoundrels and ne'er do wells, then I would ne'er completely embrace and walk fully in the gifts of my people!"

After a few minutes of this, when the story of the dream seemed to have wound its way out, I looked Kimberley in the eyes and asked, "Are you aware that you are speaking in an Irish brogue?"

Her face registered a moment of confusion and as she replied, "What? What do you mean?" the accent unraveled from her speech. In the years since, I have never heard her speak in a voice or affect an accent in any way similar.

If you're having a hard time believing this story, I don't blame you. I witnessed it in person, and I still blink my eyes and shake my head when I recall the episode. As participants in a culture built on the Western values of logic and the scientific method, we are accustomed to questioning the truth of such inexplicable experiences.

I am a big fan of the practicality of the disciplines of logic and science, both of which align with the expression of the masculine-assertive. But I have also come to accept and appreciate the ways in which sacred ceremonies, dreams, and stories can open us to the teachings of our unconscious. The transmission of sacred stories, the lessons of the dreamtime, and the keeping of sacred ceremonies are functions of the inspired receptive and as such are the domains of the feminine.

Kimberley and I learned and healed a lot together and along the way shared moments of hilarity and periods of profound happiness. Although she was at times plagued by anxiety and the lingering effects of a traumatic experience in her childhood, she had a highly developed sense of humor, which I sensed helped her to cope but also made being with her a lot of fun.

Some of our most enjoyable times together were vacations spent traveling with the kids. Kim liked to plan grand adventures with underwater caving and canyons and jungles and ziplines. Even though these experiences legitimately terrified her, she would do her best not to let on because she wanted the kids to be fearless and enjoy life in all the ways she couldn't.

We learned to expose our liabilities and vulnerabilities to each other and to take responsibility for our wounds and weaknesses. We created positive intentions and visions and worked very hard at healing old injuries and letting go of unhealthy patterns. We hurt each other, cried together, and learned to recover together. Ours was a rich relationship, one worthy of celebration, and we celebrated it with abandon and tremendous gratitude in a formal wedding ceremony.

Eventually, however, our transformational relationship brought us to a crossroads. We found through much soul-searching that over our years together we'd established certain unhealthy patterns of relating. There were ways we had unconsciously been using the relationship as a means for avoiding the deepest individual work we needed to do to address our oldest fears and heal our most tender wounds. Kimberley sensed intuitively and intensely that we would not be able to release these unhealthy dynamics while remaining in our marriage. I wasn't convinced but eventually I saw her assessment was correct; the patterns were deep, and our boundaries with each other had become muddy.

The breakup of this relationship shattered and humbled me. And the grief of this loss did what grief does. It forced me into the unfamiliar terrain of stillness, reflection, and intense feeling; it introduced me to the vast range of my own emotional landscape. It also opened me to an increased capacity for receiving and extending profound gifts of compassion. And it deepened my embodied sense of connection to those who have truly loved and lost. In other words, it threw me into the deep end of my own feminine-receptive expression.

I wasn't going to think my way out of this one. None of our most valued cultural tools for success have validity in the murky, unpredictable realms of grief. Yes, we can go to therapy, we can throw ourselves into our work, we can make plans for our next stage of life, and we can celebrate and be grateful for the good times. But, absent the necessary stillness, reflection, and space for holding and processing our feelings, none of those "activities" will alleviate the pain of such a loss. Grief requires that we surrender and make space for its intensity, its waves of sadness, and its teachings.

Many, myself included, describe becoming aware of a piercing sort of beauty in the territory of grief. I'd describe this beauty as the intersection of immense sadness for what was lost, immense gratitude for what was known, intense awareness of our vulnerability to losses to come, and tremendous compassion for self and for others who have had and will experience similar losses. Grief has a singular way of piercing the heart with the simultaneous awareness of both our individuality and our connection to all other humans.

Wrecking Myself

I didn't recognize the voice on the other end of the line. "Hi, I'm with your son. He's been in an accident, and he wanted me to call you. He's conscious, and I think he's going to be okay. But it was kind of a bad one…his car went off the road and rolled a few times. The ambulance is here now, and they are taking him to the emergency room."

Feeling my eyes stinging and a panic rising in my chest, I pulled the car off the road to get my bearings. Haley, then 13, and Grant, age 10, were in the car with me. Jesse, now attending college, had been driving himself to meet us at my cousin's house in central Louisiana. We had coordinated a road trip convergence there for a little surprise 75th birthday party and cookout for my dad.

I shook off my panic, asked for the location of the hospital, reset my navigation, and immediately got back on the road. A few minutes later, Jesse called me from the emergency room. He sounded fine, so I asked what had happened. He told me that he wasn't sure but maybe a problem with the brakes. I am embarrassed to say this answer irritated me. I knew the brakes on that car were good, and I was a little annoyed he wasn't trying harder to help me put the pieces together to determine what happened. I wanted this whole thing to make sense.

In retrospect, I think I wanted there to be a good, preventable reason for the wreck, and I wanted him to know what it was and to explain it clearly. Rather than taking these moments on the phone to empathize with him and share my relief...rather than holding space for his emotional reaction to a terrifyingly close brush with death...I grilled him. I fired a series of questions at him about all his decisions leading up to the accident.

Because of how normal he had sounded on the phone, when I walked into the hospital I expected to see my son sitting in a chair ready to leave with us. The sound of his voice calling for me from the room we'd just passed stopped me in my tracks. I hadn't recognized him.

He was propped up in the bed, his hair and face still covered in dried blood. I froze momentarily, horrified, mentally replaying the conversation I'd had with him and knowing in my heart the wrongness of it. I realized how close I'd come to losing him. Feeling my face burning and tears welling up, I willed them back down. The ER nurses were joking around with him, but they were still monitoring him closely, checking his pupils and limiting his movement.

I was struck both by their skill and their gentleness. Worried about possible injuries to his neck and back, they'd cut off his jeans before taking him into x-ray. Quite miraculously, it turned out his injuries were minor. They stapled the cut in his head, cleaned him up, and released him.

Relieved and grateful, I sprang back into action. I drove Jesse and the kids to my cousin's house, helped pull dinner together for my dad's birthday, went to fill Jesse's prescriptions and buy him some pajamas, washed the party dishes, and got the kids settled into bed. I maintained a similar level of activity throughout the weekend, going to a nearby department store to purchase Jesse a winter coat and a few other things that could have waited. I dealt with the insurance company. I arranged a visit to the tow lot to retrieve Jesse's backpack and other belongings from the startling crumple that once was his car.

All those things needed to be done, but with time I realized how out of balance my reaction was throughout the weekend. Even though I had, by then, been on a journey to reconnect with my emotional expression for years, in times of stress I still found myself reverting to old patterns.

At no point during or after the weekend did I sit with my son and allow him the space to express and discharge the fear and trauma associated with experiencing such a close brush with death. After the accident, I never allowed my presence and compassion to comfort us both and the others around us. I did not hold his hand and invite him to tell me the story of what happened while I listened and received it without critique or analysis. We all did what we did without the nurturing and emotional presence of the feminine-receptive expression.

The week following the accident, after reflecting more deeply, I wrote in my journal:

> *Jesse could die at any time by a terrible car accident or a million other possible tragedies. Any of us can. And no amount of me running around doing stuff is going to change that fact. I am intentionally sitting in that knowing right now and feeling*

it with all of my heart. And as I do this, I find myself in very deep gratitude for the kindness that has been shown to me all weekend by everyone from the young man who stopped to help my son, to my dad and my cousin's family, to the doctors and nurses in the ER, to the women in the 24-hour Walgreen's, to the sweet tow yard guys, to my partner and my community of friends, and to all three of my big-hearted kids. There has been a palpable sense of tenderness in so many of my interactions since the accident.

I wonder if I am tender enough. And I mean it. I wonder this with compassion for myself and I hold an intention to live more from my heart. I allow myself to feel connected with every parent who has lost a child or is afraid of losing a child. And I allow myself to know that it isn't just about children. This thread of fear and ache goes on and on to anyone who has ever lost anyone or is afraid of losing anyone. And I hold myself still in this place. And I hold myself still in these feelings.

Anger-Abstract in Acrylic

I felt myself suppress a grimace as Haley got out her paints and brushes and set up her art station on the kitchen table. She loved expressing herself through lines, shapes, and colors. She enjoyed recreating scenes from her life experiences and experimenting with more abstract creative concepts. She sometimes combined paint, pictures, and words into beautiful and personal collages as thoughtful gifts for her friends.

I loved this aspect of who she was and I fought hard with myself internally at times like this. I wanted so very badly to be the kind of mom who encouraged and made space for art explorations. I *desperately* did.

I wanted to relax and enjoy watching Haley's art process evolve without the grip in my gut. Instead, I felt physically anxious, wishing for the whole thing to be over and done with even before it started.

I loved going to museums and art exhibits, but when my kids picked up a paintbrush or a lump of clay, it always felt like another thing looming on my to-do list. I know in my heart that art is sacred, but my practical impulse to discourage activities that would create a mess in the house always seemed to override my reactions. I knew I was repeating a pattern from my own childhood with my own busy mom, and this was the pattern I was struggling to break.

My voice thick with this inner struggle, I cautioned, "Make sure you put newspaper down to keep from getting paint on the table." Haley was sensitive and careful. She always put newspaper down first, and she always cleaned her brushes and put her supplies away afterward. "You will need to have it all put away before dinner." It wasn't even close to dinner time.

I walked out of the room and squinted in frustration with myself, realizing I was in no way managing to contain my reaction. I still deeply regret that this was the best I could do.

It would be easy enough to attribute this tension and my associated crappy reaction to my concern that my children's art activities would interrupt my plans for getting things done and create additional work for me. The laundry and meals alone could keep me running all weekend. But somehow that reason didn't seem substantial enough to explain the intensity of my feelings. So I continued to hold and examine my responses; I have since come to a more intimate understanding of them.

At some point, early in my personal journey, I learned to suppress the aspiring young artist inside myself. I taught myself that I shouldn't waste time and energy creating drawings or singing songs, that my time would be better spent on "more valuable, practical, less messy activities." So without realizing it, in interactions like this one with Haley, I was externalizing the old argument still underway within myself.

The artistic aspect of my young self, down but apparently not out, both advocated for and envied my children's art experiments. So the scrappy little artist in me was responsible for the knots in my stomach as I made efforts to overcontrol my environment at the expense of my kids' artistic expression.

Witnessing their activities had apparently re-triggered my own inner artist's passion to fight for space for her own artistic expression. I realized most of the tension I experienced was a result of having to put down my own internal insurgence.

By now it won't surprise you to hear that, as a parent, I tended to be much more of a taskmaster and scheduler than I was a nurturer and feeler. I wanted to do parenting right, of course, but for years I thought that meant lots of directing and hard boundaries.

Toys should be picked up and put away when I said they should, not in 15 minutes. Homework needed to be done before games. Dessert was eaten after dinner. There was little space for negotiation and little time for options. I experienced my children's younger years managing myself through various levels of being overwhelmed. Although I was affectionate and did my best to express my love consistently, as the art story illustrates, I could become frustrated by the ways my kids tended to interrupt and derail my efforts to "get all the parenting things done."

I was "doing motherhood" the best I could, but I was missing half of the experience of mothering.

My relationships with my children gave me ample opportunities to see and become conscious of the pain that my unbalanced approach to parenting could create. The truth is, my kids didn't really need as many rules or boundaries as I gave them. In hindsight, I can see they all needed more listening, more emotional engagement, and more space for their creative activities and experiments than I gave them. I consider myself very lucky that while my kids all cared about doing the right things, they didn't seem particularly afraid of me.

They let me know when they thought I was going too far. While they trusted my intentions and my love, they graciously let me know, each according to their own style, when my focus was off.

Jesse argued with me to the point of exhaustion. Grant lectured me, refusing to comply until I came up with a "good enough" reason. Even gentle Haley huffed and fumed while complying with my directives. They showed me the error of trying to keep their territory, their range of expression, small enough that I could effectively "manage it." I am not saying I gave up easily. I didn't. But, slowly, I began to listen more deeply and receive the truth in the messages they were giving me.

I am grateful for the ways in which they taught me balance and the ways in which they continue to do so.

CHAPTER 3

Who Knows What Beauty

Out of Balance: Functionality and Practicality

We hurt from the lack of inspiration in our systems. Biased as our culture is toward action, accumulation, and individual achievement (the masculine-assertive expression), we undervalue the receptive experiences of beauty, inspiration, and the connection of community in our lives.

Our systems are not designed to consider or give weight to such things; we consider them optional, indulgent, and luxurious. We are taught to value functionality, efficiency, and practicality above all. Even our western models and approaches to psychology and therapy teach the primacy of practicality—consider the often-referenced Maslow's Hierarchy of Needs. This hierarchy describes five categories of human needs that dictate human behavior. The theory suggests that until the practical needs at the bottom of the pyramid are met (e.g., food, water, warmth, and safety), humans have no motivation for the presumably less essential needs: love and friendship (midway up the pyramid) and "self-actualization," which includes "creative activities" (at the top of the pyramid).

According to Maslow's model, humans are expected to have no capacity for caring about experiences of love, beauty, and art until we have first completely covered our practical needs. The bias toward the masculine-assertive is very clear in this model, which presumes a linear, logical progression of human development and regards love and beauty and community as "nice to haves."

When we can afford the cost or the time, we schedule music, dance, and other art events into our calendars. If we cannot afford these activities, they are simply ignored and regarded as not essential.

Frequently, our workspaces are designed, arranged, and outfitted to minimize cost and maximize productivity and efficiency, with little consideration for aesthetics and inspiration.

Once or twice a year while on vacation—assuming we can afford the luxury of taking one—we may visit the majesty of nature, but in our attempts to cram as many activities as possible into our brief time away, we never allow ourselves to settle in and experience the visceral and emotional fullness of her beauty. We don't allow ourselves to walk barefoot feeling the warmth of a red rock canyon or to fall asleep to the sounds and smells of an old growth forest. Heck, most of us don't even visit the local park, and when we do we fill our time there with activities, rather than taking in and enjoying the natural world.

Communities with the means to do so advocate, emphasize, and provide funding to our schools to support educational programming for the subjects of science, technology, and math. These subjects are considered objectively valuable because they are practical and may be seen as applicable to future employment. Simultaneously, we cut budgets and programs in the areas of the expressive and visual arts: the subjects that engage our human emotions, lift our spirits, and inspire us creatively.

In our consistent tendency to prioritize the importance of the "practical," we've simply forgotten the other half of who we are. The visual arts show us our inner and outer realities and illuminate our most inspiring possibilities. Dance and drama integrate emotional expression, relationships, and creative problem-solving in the movement of the physical body. Do we really want to teach math, science, technology—and even English—as merely logical and rational pursuits working in service of our most practical and reasonable ideas?

Who knows what beauty could be welcomed into being through the nurturing of more alive—more completely expressed—humans. While it's true that math, science, and technology provide us tremendously useful avenues for problem-solving, the expressive arts make our most noble aspirations visible and tangible and teach us the capacity for imagining how we might move together into a more beautiful and inspiring future. In other words, *the arts show us the problems and challenges most worth solving.*

Practices:
Beauty and Inspiration

We sometimes forget that we are born with the capacity for embodying, creating, and appreciating beauty. We are surrounded by marketing messages that tell us that beauty is expensive and that we are not capable of making our homes and environments beautiful without professional help.

If we can afford to do so, we may hire a decorator or else flip through magazines for carefully appointed and decorated homes and do our best to replicate that style in our own space. Or we may instead simply ignore the idea of beauty at home, either because we feel we cannot afford the luxury or because it feels like an unproductive waste of time. But we are, in fact, wired to sense beauty and are moved by it. We know it when we feel it.

Create a sacred space in your home. Select an item that you love, something with cherished meanings and associations, and begin there. Perhaps you have something that was passed down to you from an ancestor, a memento from a beloved friendship, or a stone or a shell saved from a favorite family beach vacation. Place the item on a small shelf or corner table along with a few candles. Allow the space around it to evolve slowly. Over time, sense what else might belong there and add it. Perhaps, a childhood photo, a feather from your morning walk, or a clay bowl that you've had for years suddenly feels like it belongs there. Keep it simple. Light the candles at least a few times a week and notice your feelings about the space. Notice any changes in your experience of the room.

As our lives get busy and hectic, we may begin to select our creative projects based on what we can complete in small time increments. Even worse, we may stop engaging with creative projects altogether because we "don't have time." Our cultural bias toward the achievement of goals and outcomes can prevent us from enjoying the mystery and discovery inherent in engaging with a creative process over a long, or uncertain, period of time. Great enjoyment can come from simply engaging with a long-term creative process without an end date or a clear design for the end product.

Create slowly. Start a project that engages you creatively and is impossible to hurry. Plant and tend a garden, even if it is on your apartment patio or in a window box, without designing it first. Start with a small selection of whatever plants and flowers appeal to you and put them wherever feels right. Over time, add to the garden in the same way. Don't hesitate to move plants around to different places.

Paint a large mural one piece at a time, without an idea for the whole. Write stories from your life, without planning a book. Savor each moment of the creative process, allowing the magic to unfold slowly by your hands. Set no goals for completion. Instead, take pictures at regular intervals and savor the evolution over time.

Artistic expression provides a way for us to tune in to the inspiration that lives inside us all and to bring it out in the world to be shared with those around us. Inspiration is by its very nature a feminine process; flashes of inspiration come to us in moments of openness and receptivity. We do not "do" inspiration.

Inspiration alone, however, is not enough to make art happen. In order to bring a new creation into being, we also must engage our masculine aspect. We must take action with the paints or the pencil or take the stage and bring that inspiration into the physical world. This balance of the feminine and masculine expressions involved in the process of creating art reminds us how to engage the fullness of our expression in the other aspects of our lives. In this way, making art reminds us how to live. And so it is that the artists in our midst—the dancers, the poets, the painters—show us the way home to ourselves.

As an adult, I had lost touch with the artist in me and convinced myself that I wasn't artistic. I only recently found my way back to a creative art practice by making time to play and experiment with different media and releasing the idea that I needed to have a "fixed goal" or specific product as an outcome. I allow myself to play with poetry and collage and sewing and give myself full permission to follow my curiosity, creative impulse, and inspiration—and to see what happens. Sometimes the outcome is a completed art piece. Sometimes the outcome is simply the feeling of being more fully alive.

Create art. Take up painting, guitar, welding, sewing, dance, drama…pick any medium that calls to you. If you get stuck on one, try another. As adults, we are most comfortable doing things we're already good at. Allow yourself to be a beginner artist and play in an artistic medium just as a child would. For a while, minimize your exposure to formal instruction and allow yourself to experiment with a free flow of inspiration. Sing without knowing what words will come. Write free association poetry right after waking. Weld the next piece without knowing what piece comes after. Fall in love with the process of creation, unattached to the outcome. BONUS: Identify a local artist whose work you admire and support her or him; attend a gallery opening; visit and blog about his or her work; or support the artist as a patron or a collector, even with just the purchase of a single print.

Not Buying In

In my early forties, I was leading and growing a small consulting and digital media company in Houston. I told myself, and anyone else who would listen, that I wanted the company to be a model of collaboration and cooperation. And because I believed myself, I decided to engage my team in a collaborative visioning process.

My approach was to invite each person to write down their answers to certain questions pertaining to how the company should be described five years into the future. My plan was to take away and integrate those ideas into a draft of our shared vision, to present it back to the team for more input and refinement, and then to finalize it so it could serve as a guidepost for how we would make decisions and do business going forward. When I look back at the way I designed this process, I can see that I absolutely wanted the visioning process to be collaborative. I also realize I had no idea how to foster collaboration. I had not even begun to understand its value.

It would be years before I'd come to know the alchemy of true collaboration. Honestly, I had to get it wrong a lot. In our culture, we have neither a shared value for deep listening nor the tools to engage a group in a process of collective inspiration and co-creation. I eventually came to know the power of real collaboration through experiences outside of traditional or conventional western contexts. I learned from elders who remembered ancient ways, I learned from artists, and I learned incrementally from my own experiments.

I'd been taught the linear and logical processes of group work. I knew how to work with a team to clarify the goal and success criteria, brainstorm and analyze alternatives, and drive to consensus. I'd learned well the perspective and the useful tools of the practical masculine-assertive. But I'd not yet learned how to align a group and set intention to establish a field of deep receptivity, curiosity, and integration in which better possibilities could spontaneously emerge from the collective wisdom; I was missing the critical perspective and connective tools of the feminine-receptive expression.

In the collaboration model that I'd experienced in school and work contexts, someone in the group already had the solution, the best answer. So the goal of collaborating was really just to identify which person had the best solution and align the group on actions to support it. In my example of the company vision, I strongly believed I knew the business best and, beyond a few tweaks, I really didn't need much input. But I did want my team to join me in the vision I had in mind, so I set a collaborative process in motion primarily for this reason.

Today this approach is called "getting buy-in." To be fair to myself, I was not totally aware of this as my motivation. I did read, consider, and discuss all of the team's responses to the visioning questions, but I mostly filtered out the ones that didn't align with the direction I saw for the company. Of course, my team noticed. Consciously or unconsciously, people sense such things. And, unsurprisingly, they never fully engaged with, owned, or shared the company vision I brought forward.

So while I had been extolling the virtues of collaboration for many years, and I legitimately believed what I was saying, it is only recently that I have experienced the co-creative power of true collaboration.

The possibilities of true collaboration are powerful because the process generates a creative field that allows the diverse gifts and perspectives of every individual in a group to emerge and contribute toward more complete solutions to challenging problems. Real collaboration involves a balance of the feminine energies of receptivity, inspiration, and integration and the masculine energies of assertion, action, and construction. Real collaboration holds the potential to enable us to generate more holistic, sensitive systems that are more inclusive, more balanced, and more life-affirming.

Panting with Strangers

My friend, Suzanne, has surprised me many times over the years, always challenging and inspiring me with the ways in which she engages the world and often leading me to try new things.

"I signed you up for yoga," she said through a wry smile and with a slight strain in her voice. She was doing that thing that long-time smokers do so skillfully, speaking while continuing to hold the smoke in her lungs.

After a pause and a head tilt, I replied, "What do you mean you signed me up for yoga?"

She politely blew the smoke out of the corner of her mouth waving it off to the side with her hand, "I mean, the class is at the Jewish Community Center next door to your house, and I figured we could go together, so I signed you up, too.... You *said* you wanted to take yoga."

She had me there. In the several months since I'd returned from my solo San Francisco trip, I'd been talking about wanting to learn yoga but hadn't done anything about it. Laughing, I agreed to go on the condition that she teach me how to hold a cigarette. (I'd never wanted to smoke, but I'd always been curious about how it felt to hold one and flick the ashes while gesturing dramatically.)

The instructor entered the classroom carrying a sheepskin and sporting a full beard, a white turban, and a white kurta with matching pants. He carefully squatted at the front of the class, placed the sheepskin on the floor by his feet, and seated himself upon it cross-legged. Smiling sweetly and without introduction, he began to teach, inviting us to follow his lead in a pose from the same seated and cross-legged position he had taken. The first posture involved gripping the fingers to the palms and pointing the thumbs to the sky, making a V with the elbows locked out and the arms extended at 45-degree angles from the vertical line of the body. He proceeded to teach us a breath exercise (*pranayama*) called "breath of fire," which involves rapid and deep inhales and exhales through the nose, all controlled from the belly.

As we strove to continue this rapid breathing for several minutes, our instructor good naturedly encouraged us to "keep up" and provided instructions for what to do if we felt lightheaded (slow down the breath and balance the inhales with the exhales) or felt we couldn't continue (maintain the posture while taking a break from the breathing). Now I didn't know yoga, but I could already tell this wasn't *normal* yoga. This was, as it turned out, not only my very first yoga class, it was my first *kundalini* yoga class.

Most yoga classes taught in the US are some variation of hatha yoga. Hatha yoga is to kundalini yoga as a lawnmower is to a bonfire. Hatha yoga, as it's usually taught in the West, has a broad focus on the consistent development of general flexibility and awareness, and most Americans approach it more as a fitness or stress relief regime than as a way of growing consciousness.

By contrast, kundalini yoga brings a tremendous intensity of focus to certain aspects of awareness. In a kundalini yoga class, instructions typically include a combination of posture, physical movements, breath patterns, eye focus, hand positions (mudras), and chants (mantras). There are literally hundreds of different combinations documented, and each combination is intended to activate certain specific aspects of awareness and healing.

Getting the combinations right can require seemingly near impossible levels of focus and coordination, and the instructors typically teach a different yoga set, or *kriya*, every class. This means that a part of what long-time students of this form of yoga come to expect is that we will simply remain bad at yoga...pretty much forever. In a real way, part of the practice is learning to stay with the effort and intention in spite of that expectation.

The active part of the kriya is generally followed by a meditation. Kundalini yoga meditations involve quieter, less active combinations of mudras, mantras, and instructions for the eyes and the point of focus. After the meditation, students are instructed to lie on their backs in *Savasana* (corpse pose) and "integrate" the benefits of the yoga set.

Through much of the first class, I cut a series of incredulous raised eyebrow side-eye glances to Suzanne, as if to say, "How did you manage to sign us up for the weirdest damn yoga class in the city?"

I was not adequately prepared for loud panting with strangers or chanting words in an ancient language through bizarre sets of calisthenics with my eyes one-tenth open and my attention focused at my "third eye." But at the end of the class, as I lay on my back, I felt a swirl of unfamiliar sensations pulsing through and around my body.

I would describe these feelings as a kind of electricity in the space around my hands and feet and an intense concentration of heat in my abdomen. And none of it was static or familiar in any way. I'd been athletic and physically active all my life. I knew what a "cool down" felt like with its slow and predictable descent of intensity. This wasn't that. This felt more like a mild internal electrical storm.

My intellect kept trying to attribute these sensations to blood flow or lactic acid or endorphins, but something deeper in me knew this was a very different sort of experience than any I'd had previously. Even though the whole experience had felt inexplicably strange to me, my curiosity had been piqued; I seldom missed a class. Once that program ended, I signed myself up for the next session of classes. And then the next. My breath of fire technique improved dramatically, but I never did manage to look natural or cool in any way, holding a cigarette.

Although it was a slow start, the yoga experience was one of my first steps toward a more intentional approach to experimentation in my life.

Head Banging and Kriyas Crossing

The following year, Sat Kartar, the bearded teacher with the sheep-skin, handed out flyers announcing a kundalini yoga teacher train-ing program in Houston. I signed up immediately, without com-pletely knowing why. I was learning to follow my instincts and intuitions on such things, and this opportunity just felt like a "yes" in my body so I followed it.

I was in my mid-thirties when I began this intensive yoga teacher training program, and what happened next marked an-other turning point in my life, opening me to powerful new ex-periences and a deeper understanding of the ways in which the physical body could be engaged to accelerate healing and personal transformation.

At the time, I'd been meeting regularly for a couple of years with a counselor in traditional talk therapy sessions; I'd been ex-amining and attempting to release certain old, unhealthy patterns of communication and relating. I had not by then gone very deep, so none of these patterns was particularly earth-shattering. They were fairly common issues like learning to recognize and express my needs directly, rather than hoping they would be seen and met without my asking or advocacy. I was also working to release my inevitable passive-aggressive response to situations in which my unspoken needs were not met.

I had an excellent therapist who helped me unpack and analyze these old patterns and recognize the triggers, but I was still finding them difficult to release. I just couldn't seem to get ahead of them and interrupt them. Understanding the patterns, it seemed, was not enough; it felt as if they were somehow lodged in me, programmed into my reactions. Over and over, I fell into the old programs automatically and unconsciously and was only able to recognize and analyze them in retrospect.

So it startled me one day when suddenly I found myself with the time and space to make a different choice in a situation in which it would have been easy to slide into old patterns. One of my old habits was to deflect pain or embarrassment with a sarcastic or cutting comment directed at someone else. That reaction, which I'd internalized as a child, would take the focus off me and serve as my first line of defense against unpleasant feelings. From there, I usually could wrest control over the situation or dynamic and take it in a different direction that felt "safer" or easier for me to manage. This old reaction was as instant and impulsive as it was corrosive, and I'd been working to release it for years. When this shift happened, I found myself able to intercept the impulse and just sit quietly for a moment, allowing the awareness of my discomfort. It wasn't easy, but for the first time, it was possible.

I recognized the moment as a breakthrough, thinking, "Oh, it's about time. I guess this is how therapy works…you bang your head against the wall for a couple of years and then, boom, the old programming releases." Reenergized, I doubled down on my work in therapy, identifying and beginning to unpack the next layers of my issues with my counselor. I fully expected it would be another couple of years before I would be able to make any noteworthy progress in circumventing or releasing them. Instead, I found myself able to recognize the situations and triggers as they were emerging, often in time to interrupt the patterns and change my response. For reasons I didn't understand, I was experiencing a dramatic acceleration in my personal growth work.

I felt my mind working overtime to understand this acceleration. Was I simply maturing? Had that first breakthrough created a new set of neural connections, establishing a new and faster pattern for transformation that was now embedded in my consciousness? I knew this was a code worth cracking, and I toyed with all sorts of possibilities.

Then one evening, as I lay on my back in Savasana at the end of a full day of yoga teacher training, I had a realization: my breakthroughs in therapy began almost simultaneously with the beginning of my yoga teacher training program.

In fact, the first breakthrough happened in the midst of an intense assignment we were each given to select a specific kriya and practice it every day for 40 days in a row. I had chosen *Sodarshan Chakra Kriya*, a very challenging yoga set.

I wondered, "Could it be the combination of talk therapy and the kundalini yoga practice that had accelerated my work in therapy?" I began to hold that possibility in my mind and test it against my experience.

I began to bring a different level of attention to my yoga practice and classes. I pored over the descriptions of the hundreds of yoga sets, or kriyas, in my kundalini yoga books seeking to understand how they worked. Each one is focused on developing, healing, or balancing a different aspect of consciousness. For example, there are certain kriyas that focus on awakening and developing the capacity for both expressing and receiving love and compassion, there are kriyas that focus on releasing addictive thoughts and actions, and there are others that target the development of awareness and consciousness in communication (both expressive and receptive).

The list is comprehensive and covers everything from improving digestion to removing blocks to prosperity. The deeper I dug into the study and practice of the various kriyas, the more I came to recognize the significance of the combinations of breathwork, postures, and the physical movements throughout each of the kriyas.

The physical shapes and movements in Kundalini yoga mirror and emphasize the intended focus of each kriya. For example, the movements in kriyas for strengthening the capacity for love and compassion often involve hands placed over the heart, postures and movements that look like a repeated self-embrace, postures that require the practitioner to hold the chest open receptively and vulnerably for several minutes, and movements that begin at the chest and seem to simulate the way it would look if it were possible to literally push love out into the world from there. Similarly, the kriyas for strengthening communication involve intense breathwork, movements to loosen the spine and release points of tension, receptive V-shaped postures, and chants to engage and activate the vocal chords.

I began to embrace the idea that the daily practice of kundalini yoga accelerated my personal growth and healing work in talk therapy. Having now practiced this style of yoga for over 20 years, I have no idea where, who, or how I'd be without it.

These practices have been the ratchet and socket set in my life-survival toolkit. They've equipped me to target and activate areas of growth, provided me with methods to reawaken the feminine-receptive aspect of my expression and balance it with the masculine-assertive aspect, and enabled me to work through periods of anxiety, depression, and grief. At times, I still drop unconsciously into some of the same old patterns that plagued me back then; transformation is not a straight line. The difference now is that I don't *always* drop into them, and when I do I have methods for getting myself back on track.

Having experienced the power of moving differently through yoga, I began running all kinds of experiments on myself, experiments that required me to move my physical body in unfamiliar ways, often in ways and places well outside my comfort zone.

Ways Without Maps

"Right or left?" I asked as Kimberley and I came into the intersection.

"Right," she pointed.

"Yeah, I'm feeling that too." As we made the turn away from San Marcos, I wondered where we might end up.

We started this road trip around noon, and we'd been driving for about three hours. We continued navigating in this way, making turns whenever it felt good to do so. We'd been experimenting with intuitive driving for a year or so but had never previously packed our bags for an overnight road trip. The route was a scenic one, and we took our time, stopping along the way to investigate little antique shops and find good French fries.

By the time we arrived in San Marcos, we both anticipated the journey would end there with us finding a little hotel or bed and breakfast in this sweet, green college town. But after looping around the city, neither of us felt it was time to stop. So we continued driving, taking what looked to be an unpromising turn away from the land of cute coffee shops and easy lodging.

About 20 minutes later, after another exit and a few turns, we arrived in the town of Wimberley, an artsy little getaway with antique and vintage shops, small galleries, tree-lined streets, and a very friendly set of locals. We'd both heard of Wimberley and knew it to be a cute and campy place for a weekend retreat, but we'd never visited.

Kim and I looked at each other and high-fived, agreeing we'd found our destination for the evening. We wanted to get settled and look around a bit before dinner, so we started looking for lodging. Kim was driving, so I scribbled down phone numbers and began making calls to local inns and bed and breakfasts to ask about vacancies. After a handful of unsuccessful attempts, it became clear we had arrived on a busy weekend.

We weren't about to give up easily, and at the edge of town we took another intuitive right turn onto a narrow, gravel road that ran alongside a scenic creek. We saw a sign for a lodge and hoped we might find ourselves in luck. Less than a mile down the road, I noticed a pink granite stone marker next to an entry drive.. We slowed to check it out. On the surface was engraved the word, "Abundance" along with a phone number.

I laughed and looked at Kimberley. The sign marked the entrance to the site of two gorgeous and beautifully landscaped rental cabins in a wooded area. We pulled over and I dialed the number. No one answered, so I left a message on the voicemail with my callback information. Then I declared matter-of-factly, "Okay, good. We're staying here."

Kim looked at me as if I were crazy and shook her head, "There's no way they aren't booked."

I smiled and replied, "Let's just park the car and take a stroll down by the creek because they are about to call us back and tell us we can stay here."

Skeptical but amused by my confidence, she agreed, and we made our way down through the shady canopy of live oaks and pines and thready cypress trees to wander alongside the creek.

About 10 minutes into the walk, my phone rang. I shot Kimberley a smirk and answered with a dramatic flourish. "Hello, is this Tina?" said the voice on the other end.

"Yes, it is!" I replied happily, sensing from her tone that we were in luck. But it was even better than that. "I can't believe this!" the voice exclaimed, "This is Tina Sabuco from Houston! You have found our cabins in Wimberley!"

It took my mind a second to catch up with what was happening. I'd known Tina and her partner Shellye for more than 10 years, and I'd seen them in social situations but never learned they had cabins in this area.

"We had a last-minute cancellation," she continued, "so we'll let you stay there for a song!" Not only had we driven intuitively to a popular and lovely retreat town but we'd also found a last-minute vacancy in a beautifully appointed cabin that was owned by friends in Houston. This is, I was learning, the sort of magic that can happen when you follow the intuition of the feminine-receptive.

Learning to move this way opens possibilities for joyful chance encounters and adventures. I was still new to this intuitive way of moving, but I was beginning to love it. We have plans. We have schedules. We follow them for the sake of efficiency and time management. But what happens when we don't? I have often found that it is magic and serendipity and new friends and art and surprises and delight and coffee shops and books. I have experienced so many spontaneous high points of joy and connection in my life by opening the door and making space for my intuition to play. Intuition dwells in the realm of the feminine-receptive, and if we learn to listen it will lead us to know days rich with inspiration and lives rich with possibilities.

Lost Cause to Chaos

The instructor pointed to the dance floor and invited me to get warmed up. Dance classes were not the norm for me, and I didn't really know how to "warm up." I quickly scanned the room to see if I could take some cues from the others. An older man with a long ponytail was stretching out his back on a large exercise ball. A woman was sort of twirling and bounding around and would occasionally stop and reach for the floor. I shuffled self-consciously to the back of the room, sat on the floor, and started doing some yoga stretches—hoping if I was doing something wrong, the instructor would run a gentle intervention.

I'd dropped in to this Saturday morning 5Rhythms dance class on the recommendation of a Seattle DJ/dancer friend because I was committed to experimenting with different ways of moving… and apparently to making myself very uncomfortable.

Once our (smaller than expected) group of eight had gathered and stretched awhile, Tammy, the instructor, bounced lightly over to the sound system and started the music for "flowing." Flowing is the first of the five rhythms.

She gave us very little instruction for how to dance this rhythm, saying only that flowing is led by the feet, that the feet are allowed to glide around wherever they want to go, with the rest of the body taking their direction. For a while, I pondered what it meant to allow my feet to lead. It didn't help that no one's "flow" looked even remotely like anyone else's. Ponytail guy's flow looked a lot like hopping and bouncing all over the room, and twirly woman's flow was, well, twirly…and backwards. So I was never able to figure out if I was flowing "correctly" or not.

Then abruptly, it seemed to me, Tammy changed the music to move us into the second rhythm, called "staccato."

"In staccato," she explained, "we let the hips lead."

Well, my hips can be fairly introverted in groups, so it took a little convincing to get them to take the reins in any sort of obvious way. And then, mercifully, we got a little more instruction from Tammy, explaining that the staccato rhythm invokes a confident intentional sort of emergent movement. My mind locked onto that instruction and promptly relieved my hips from duty.

In the midst of my celebration, Tammy changed the music again, moving us into "chaos," the third rhythm. The instruction was to "gently" allow the head to join the movement and to completely surrender to whatever the body wanted to do.

Chaos was by far my favorite of the rhythms. I gave up trying to learn from others and—apart from occasional glances to make sure I didn't run into anyone—my eyes remained closed. My arms flailed wildly, my hips reasserted themselves, my body changed direction without warning, my bare feet stomped loudly without regard, my head did its own thing entirely, and my mind—outnumbered and overpowered—simply surrendered.

When we were instructed to move into "lyrical," the fourth rhythm, I was sort of a lost cause to chaos. I don't actually remember the instruction for lyrical. The music took on a sort of salsa vibe, and Tammy seemed to be bringing in her hands and arms and moving them in a more coordinated and controlled way. So I did what I could to collect myself into a more contained sort of movement, but it felt a little like trying to dance while taking a couple of golden retrievers for a walk in a ball park.

By the time we got to "stillness," the fifth rhythm, I was already prone on the floor. My memory of the instruction was something that involved slowing down our movement at whatever pace felt right to us and then eventually finding our way into a place of stillness. Well, the place of stillness came immediately for me. I really loved the feeling of just lying there on the floor in surrender to what my body was telling me it needed. Surrender was beginning to become a consistent theme for me.

This experiment with the 5Rhythms provided me with a glimpse of yet another piece of the puzzle as I continued to become reacquainted with my receptive-feminine aspect.

My discomfort with the lack of direction prompted me to explore the significance of undirected time and spontaneity. I planned the hours and minutes in my days very carefully. And even though I had allocated the time to experience this dance class, the experience showed me the degree to which my daily activities had become about "doing the right things at the designated times." I was unpracticed in spontaneity, unskilled at imagining or moving myself in a context absent of clear direction or instruction.

Kundalini yoga had opened me to new kinds of self-experimentation; it began my time of reaching out to explore new ways of moving and relating.

According to our cultural norms, unscheduled, unproductive time is time wasted. This norm is reinforced by the exalted hero stories of hard-working people who burned the midnight oil and bootstrapped themselves with discipline and a refusal to waste a minute. Steve Jobs reportedly told his biographer that when he returned to Apple in 1996, he worked from 7:00 a.m. to 9:00 p.m. every day.[2]

Indra Nooyi, former CEO of Pepsi, reportedly worked from midnight to 5:00 a.m. as a receptionist to earn money while getting her master's degree at Yale. She described starting a typical day

---

2   Dave Smith, "The Steve Jobs Guide to Manipulating People and Getting What You Want," Business Insider, June 2, 2019, https://www.businessinsider.com/steve-jobs-guide-to-getting-what-you-want-2016-10#being-brutally-honest-will-help-you-build-a-strong-following.

at 4:00 a.m. and often working until midnight.[3]

Undirected time is appreciated only as a brief respite and as the payoff for hard work. It is not inherently valued as a receptive opening for spontaneous inspiration, intuition, or creative problem-solving. We can see this reflected in the following quote from the well-known, self-help author, Tony Robbins:

"It's important to reward yourself, and your team, as soon as you complete a key task or objective. Why? By rewarding yourself in the moment, your brain elicits positive emotions, leading to the realization that your efforts result in a positive reward. By doing this continuously, your brain will start to link pleasure to accomplishing the task or objective and move towards it in the future." [4]

Out of Balance: Schedules, Work, and Activity

We overschedule ourselves and our families and fill our waking hours with activity, leaving less time for rest, recovery, and spontaneity. Time with our loved ones is often compressed and more focused on planned activities than on emotional presence and meaningful engagement. We measure our success by how productive we've been and by how many activities we cram into each day. This trend can leave us feeling exhausted, mentally dull, and anxious. We wear our overwork, our "grind," as a badge of honor in our unbalanced culture that values the masculine-assertive expression of "doing" over the feminine-receptive expression of "being."

We override the needs of our bodies, often sacrificing our health, in the service of doing more. Eventually we may stop noticing the

---

3   Jacquelyn Smith, "The Insane Work Ethic of Mark Cuban, Jeff Bezos, and 14 Other Powerful Leaders," Inc., April 8, 2016, https://www.inc.com/business-insider/work-ethic-of-super-successful-people.html.

4   "Celebrate Your Accomplishments the Right Way: Tony Robbins," Tony Robbins, March 6, 2020, https://www.tonyrobbins.com/productivity-performance/reward-yourself/.

needs of our bodies at all. This disassociation from the intrinsic intelligence of our bodies makes it possible for us to keep marching forward, "doing what we need to do," without full acknowledgment of how taxing this trend is to our physical and emotional well-being.

And whether we realize it or not, we are bequeathing this same bias to the next generation. We overplan and overschedule our family time as well. Denise Pope, founder of the Stanford-based educational organization Challenge Success, cautions against keeping kids overly busy with supervised activities, emphasizing the need for free, unstructured playtime for healthy development.[5]

Today, the moments families do spend together after school and work activities are likely to be spent in frantic action getting dinner on the table and making sure homework gets done before everyone falls into bed for the night. We're missing the kind of relaxed togetherness that allows for easy communication and spontaneous fun or creativity to emerge.

As much as we might be in the habit of thinking of ourselves as logical and rational persons of action, as humans we all need stillness, nurturing, communion, and emotional presence. These aspects of our being are always available to us; though they may be sleeping, they live within each of us as the feminine-receptive.

Practices:
Spontaneity, Play, and Stillness

For some of us, driving has become a tedious activity, just a way to get from point A to point B. We have a "places to be and schedules to keep and miles to go before we sleep"

---

5   Deborah Farmer Kris, "Three Things Overscheduled Kids Need More of in Their Lives," KQED, August 26, 2019, https://www.kqed.org/mindshift/54248/three-things-overscheduled-kids-needmore-of-in-their.lives.

attitude. It's easy to forget how amazing it is to be able to travel such long distances across the land in such a short period of time. Reconnect to a time, perhaps from childhood, when you had no place to be and had the freedom to explore your surroundings for no reason except to satisfy your own curiosity.

Take a morning or a day trip and just drive intuitively. No goals. No schedule. Don't decide where to go, don't use a map or any electronic devices; just get in your car and embark on a completely spontaneous adventure, turning and stopping according to your instincts. Invite a friend if you like. Decide on an initial direction, and just drive until it feels right to either stop or turn again. Trust yourself. Stop any place that catches your eye or calls to you. You are free. The wheels are yours. Use them! Make note of the ways in which this experience changes your perspective...on this day and through the following week. If you don't have a car, recreate this idea with a walk, bicycling, or even on a bus!

Our daily routines and rules to live by can be very useful. They help us stay regulated, give our days structure, and help us cover the bases of our busy lives. Sometimes, however, although our rules were made for a certain time in our lives, we continue to hold onto them out of habit, even though they are no longer necessary. For example, some retirees continue to set an alarm and wake up at the same time each day as they did when they were working full time. There's nothing wrong in doing this but it's good to be aware of our habits. Sometimes we have more flexibility than we allow ourselves.

Of course, there are times when our capacity is limited, like when starting a new business or caring for a new baby. Still, downtime is essential for rest, change, recharging—and inspiration. Inspiration doesn't happen without the time to let it emerge. Legend has it that Thomas Edison used to sit in his chair and doze off holding ball bearings in his hand; when he'd relaxed enough to drop the balls, he'd startle into alertness with some of his best ideas.

Our imaginations are fed by reverie, space, and novelty. And it's through the portal of imagination that we are inspired to open the flow of creative movement in our lives and to envision exciting new possibilities.

Take a holiday from daily rituals and break a few of your favorite personal rules. Pick one or two you're most attached to. Brush your teeth first. Miss the meeting. Eat dinner for breakfast. Wear a tie. Take a different route to work. Forget your makeup. Get dirty. Let the kids stay up late. Go to a restaurant in your pajamas. Forget to mow the lawn. Replace your Netflix time with an evening walk. Change things up and pay attention to your reactions. See what possibilities emerge when you make space for novelty.

For most of us, our minds run the show. The mind tells us what to do, when to move, when to work, when to sleep, and when and what to eat. Our cultural overbalance toward the masculine expression tells us we need to be productive and stay in action all the time. The needs and desires of our bodies are regularly overruled in favor of what the mind thinks "needs to be done" so we remain sitting and working when our bodies are screaming for us to get up and take a walk outside or to lie down for a nap.

Let your body lead. Listen to what your body says it needs, and let it run the show for a day. Take a few minutes each day to tune in deeply to the needs and wishes of your physical body. Sink into the awareness of what your body wants to do and do it. Move in the ways your body wants to move, go to the places it wants to go, free dance in the ways it wants to dance, eat the things it says it needs, skip through the park, lie down in the grass and rest. Notice and appreciate the difference.

Many of us spend our days indoors and in cars, moving according to a planned schedule, and interacting mostly with electronics and other screens. This routine contracts our life experience, overwhelms our senses, and leaves us feeling exhausted. From this state of exhaustion, it's difficult to imagine that our spirits might be fed and our bodies reenergized by an aimless walk outdoors.

Take a walk outside without your phone; wander aimlessly but mindfully. Pay attention to the combinations of colors and textures in the natural world, and notice your reactions to them. Make a point of allowing the direction of your walk to be random; try reversing or looping or zigzagging a trail. Collect a few leaves or feathers or stones and examine them closely. Sketch one or two of them in a journal or sketch pad and try to capture their most distinctive characteristics—without judging your drawing skills! Make note of where you found them and how they feel in your hands.

The daily routines of our lives serve to help us get all the things done. Over time, however, these routines can contract our range of physical movements into a small and fairly predictable repertoire of combinations.

And while we may become quite adept at the combinations, these routines can eventually result in an overall loss of flexibility in our physical bodies, reducing our range of motion.

We have come to think of this loss of flexibility as a natural result of the aging process, but it is perhaps more accurately described as a natural result of habituated movement. We literally become "set in our ways." Additionally, our physical habits tend to reinforce our mental habits; as we become less flexible physically, we also become less flexible in our thinking.

Move differently. Intentionally remind your body (and your mind by extension) that it can move in a myriad of nonroutine ways. Each day for a week, move for 15 minutes in a completely unfamiliar way that is enjoyable to you. Walk backwards (assisted), free dance in your living room, learn tai chi, go to the park and slide down the slide, roll in the grass. Slide. Crawl. Roll. Stand on your head. Work to perfect a difficult yoga posture.

Many of us live life according to what's on the "to-do" list. We like to get things done and check them off, cramming as much activity as possible into every waking hour, even when we are at home or off work on vacation. We tell ourselves we'll relax after we get enough things done but the list never ends. Inspiration requires receptivity. Receptivity requires stillness. Stillness requires…well…stopping what you're doing.

Be. Take a day off, experiencing the extreme sport of doing nothing. In stillness, you will encounter all the usual suspects that spur you into activity. Ignore them. Your list will still be there tomorrow. Try not to distract or entertain yourself. Make yourself comfortable…and be still. Remain still past the discomfort. Sit on the porch with a sketch pad and pencil, nap in the easy chair, and journal inspirations and ideas.

Our focus on action can disconnect us from some of the most important aspects of our humanity. Breathing, for example. During the colonization of Hawaii, the islanders came up with the nickname "Haole" for the mainlanders who were settling there. Haole, literally translated means "without breath." Western culture is a culture of shallow breathers. Rapid shallow breath is associated with stress, hypertension, and the "fight-or-flight" response to threats.

In his book, *Breath: The New Science of the Lost Art,* James Nestor gives many examples of the ways in which breathing assists physical and mental health.[6] The health benefits of deep breathing include stress reduction, detoxification of the blood, better concentration, and release of endorphins.

In the East, the breath is sometimes described as the vehicle for the "life force energy" or "prana." From this perspective, we can think of deep breathing as a means of increasing our receptivity to the energy of life. Nestor cites the fact that we take some 670 million breaths in our lifetime. Breathing is not only a part of our lives, it's how we live.

Go somewhere quiet where you will be uninterrupted and reacquaint yourself with your breathing. Mentally scan your physical body and notice your mental state. Set a timer for five minutes, close your eyes, and begin taking in long, deep breaths, inhaling through the nose. Fill the lungs completely, briefly suspending the breath at the top of the inhale, and then release it slowly, keeping the mouth closed and exhaling through the nose. Pay attention to any physical sensations associated with both the inhale and the

---

6 Nestor, James, *Breath: The New Science of the Lost Art,* (Riverhead Books, May 26, 2020).

exhale. After the timer goes off, take a minute to once again scan your body and mental state, making note of any differences. Also notice any shifts in your energy level, attention, and awareness. Consider incorporating five minutes of this practice as part of your daily routine.

CHAPTER 4

Escape from the Attic

Grounded by an Elder

During the early years of my relationship with Kimberley, I was taking classes toward a master's in ecopsychology at Naropa University in Boulder, Colorado. In one of my classes, I had a transformational experience while learning an ancient method for group communication.

The silver-haired woman sitting cross-legged on the floor next to me in our circle of four was speaking about her experience in apartheid South Africa. Tears filled her eyes as she told the story of her family, her regret, and her grief. Her words seemed almost material, as if the vibration of her voice and the lilt of her accent took form and moved me, physically. As she spoke, I felt her words reverberate in my own emotional and physical space; my face grew hot with her sadness, and I felt my entire body drawn down to the ground, as if I were magnetized to the earth. It felt as if the emotional resonance in her expression somehow literally "grounded me." Was it sensations like this, I wonder, that made descriptions of physicality like "touching" and "moving" commonplace in referencing emotional experiences.

We were learning a group process called "The Way of Council" or "council practice." I had volunteered myself to join the South African woman and two others in the center of the classroom. As instructed, we were demonstrating the practice in stages. Council practice employs a set of simple instructions to create a democratic, safe, emotional space, a field in which participants learn to engage in deep listening and heart-centered speaking. This teaching made me aware of how my patterns of intellectualizing showed up in my communication, and this experience taught me in a visceral way that I did not actually know how to speak from my heart in a group setting.

I felt in touch with my feelings inconsistently as it was, and I could struggle, at times, to stay with them even in a one-on-one situation. But in a group or in front of an audience, I simply didn't have access. The technique of disassociating from my emotions, which had served me so well for so long, was now getting in the way of my ability to communicate what I knew to be a more complete and powerful expression of my truth in a moment.

My Geneva Convention

A few years later, I was confronted with the same challenge in a corporate setting, a setting that consistently reinforced the old patterns I was trying to release.

I was a regular presenter at Digital Energy conferences. My presentation topics usually provided a perspective on the intersection of digital innovation in the energy industry, people, and change. My sessions were generally well attended and the feedback was positive. I knew my presentations were thoughtful and well structured, and I made a point of including practical guidance. I sensed, however, that my talks lacked the power that comes from emotional connection.

Earlier in the year, I'd been nominated by a senior member of this professional engineering organization for the designation of distinguished lecturer. If selected, over the course of the following year, I would be intermittently traveling and sharing my expertise with different chapters of this organization around the world.

This presentation before the committee was to be the final hurdle before my selection would be made official.

I began to experiment, looking for ways to connect more authentically and emotionally with my audience. But the result wasn't what I'd expected.

At my final presentation for the Society of Petroleum Engineers, as I unplugged my computer and stepped down from the podium, the head of the committee stood up abruptly and swiveled to face the others in the audience.

"I want to know who *nominated* her," he growled, his voice gripped by anger. "She has *no* business being here."

He was a short, slight man in a brown business suit with the whitest teeth I'd ever seen. I stopped in my tracks, took a deep breath to steady myself, and tucked my computer under my arm.

He continued, "Her presentation is absolutely *not* appropriate for a technical audience."

I continued to stand just at the base of the podium holding my facial expression neutral. The room was silent. A few of the men appeared shocked by his outburst. He then turned his attention to me, almost spitting his words, "I found absolutely *nothing* of value in your presentation."

At that point, a man from the audience interrupted him.

"Hang on a second," he said, his voice deferential but firm. "Her presentation is different…and maybe the material should be adjusted, but I think she brings an important perspective about how people in our industry are responding to the technology changes."

My presentation focused on the challenges related to the fact that the most experienced engineers were accustomed to working alone, while the greatest value from new digital technologies could only be realized if they embraced more collaborative ways of working and solving problems together. It was not a scientific presentation. It was, however, well-founded and I knew the content was strong. Perhaps, I allowed myself to elaborate too much or linger too long on the emotional impacts of such dramatic changes in job expectations.

The head of the committee scoffed audibly, "This is not engineering or scientific content. It is not relevant to our membership."

At the time, I ran a small consultancy in Houston, advising Fortune 500 corporations on strategies to bring on new digital toolsets and support collaborative workflows for engineers and other technical professionals in the petroleum industry. I knew my stuff, and I wasn't used to having my ass handed to me—certainly not this publicly in a professional setting.

Inside, I was utterly destroyed. But as the only woman and the only nonscientific business professional in a room full of engineers and scientists, I was determined not to fall apart.

I took a deep breath, turned to face the head of the committee, gave a little head tilt, and spoke with all the confidence I could summon from anything I'd ever felt I'd done well during my 42 years on the planet.

I knew I was the "odd duck" with my presentation focus but I had been nominated for this honor and I said so.

"Someone in your organization heard me speak at the Digital Oilfield Conference and nominated me for this program. I didn't just show up here uninvited. I went through your review process. If you feel my presentation is not appropriate, I'm a grown-up. I can handle that feedback."

While I did not consider this a particularly strong rebuttal, I was immensely proud that I managed to respond with some semblance of dignity, having choked down any evidence of my immense shame and embarrassment at such a public takedown. The presentations continued, and I managed to look engaged and interested through the final two technical sessions. I even milled about at the end of the proceedings and exchanged business cards with a couple of supportive committee members before making my escape into the brisk air and bright sunshine of Geneva, Switzerland.

It was about midday, and since I was far too disassociated from my emotions by then to cry, I decided to do a little sightseeing.

My adrenaline completely amped and now on a mission, I vigorously strode the five blocks back to my hotel, tore off my French-made business suit, and threw on my jeans and sweater, my Hello Kitty pink watch cap, and my long black wool coat before turning on my heels and heading right back out to explore the city.

Enjoying the sensation of the cold air entering my lungs, I laughed at myself, realizing I had no idea where I was or which direction to walk. But I'd learned a few things by then, and I knew how to appreciate and enjoy the mystery of not knowing.

When I allowed myself to follow the guidance of my intuition, I typically ended up in fascinating places, having amazing experiences. I took a brief moment to survey the landscape, caught a glimpse of the Jet d'Eau fountain on Geneva Lake, and began making my way toward it. I walked along the edge of the lake for a good distance, but I found myself unable to relax and enjoy the experience.

Though I was trying hard not to think about it, my mind kept returning to that moment in the auditorium and the words of the man in the brown suit, "I found absolutely *nothing* of value in your presentation."

Of course, I'd hoped the attendees would be interested in my perspective and find useful ways to apply the material, but I also had wanted the content to move them, to help them relate and empathize with the feelings of the people who were being asked to change their ways of working so dramatically.

In some part of my mind, I wanted to understand what I had missed and a few flashes of insight started to emerge. For one thing, I had deviated too much from the organization's conventions in my presentation.

At the time, I was leading my company through a strategic restart; for months, my days had been packed with meetings, contracts, and proposals. I had to admit to myself that I had not devoted enough time to familiarizing myself with the presentations of previous lecturers.

I noticed during the morning's proceedings that the flow of every presentation except mine mapped directly to the stages of the scientific method: Hypothesize, test, analyze, conclude. While my presentation material was not intended to be scientific in nature, I wondered whether it might have been met with a warmer reception had I oriented it to a similar flow. Perhaps, the head of the committee felt I had not shown adequate respect and appreciation for the honor for which I was being considered.

But there was another thing: I had gone off script. For years, I had been carefully studying the public speakers I found compelling: Maya Angelou, Tony Robbins, Marianne Williamson, and others. They had a way of showing up, a powerful presence that allowed for them to connect with their audiences well beyond the content of their presentations. They inspired people and moved people and touched the hearts of people.

I wanted desperately to learn how to connect in that way, and I'd been practicing whenever I could, often in my car and the shower. During my solitary rehearsals leading up to the presentation, I felt I could sometimes hit that groove and speak from a similar state of presence; it felt most accessible to me when I shared my personal stories, stories of my own emotional vulnerabilities and edges. And even though I knew it was risky to run this kind of experiment in a professional context, I'd decided to try it that morning in Geneva. (Oh yes, my learning style is awkward. And it's still how I learn.)

Even before my public dressing down, I knew the experiment had failed. As I'd shared my stories that morning, I sensed their flatness myself. Instead of dropping into connection and presence with my audience, I found myself locked in a state of hypervigilance, self-consciousness, and intellectualism that held me at an emotional distance. This nonemotional state was familiar to me, and in the past I had more or less made it work for the kinds of business content I typically presented.

What I'm saying is, my past presentations were never compelling or thrilling or moving...but they also weren't weird. What's weird is telling personal stories of emotional vulnerability while simultaneously being emotionally disassociated.

Unfortunately, rather than deepening the connection with my audience, sharing my personal stories without an emotional connection likely came off as if I was trying to manipulate the audience.

Squinting at the sunlight coming through the spray at the top of the fountain and coming back into the moment, I whispered to myself, "Next time, dumbass…practice with an audience."

As it turned out, I wasn't selected but several of the members approached me during a break to encourage me; they told me they would nominate me the following year and assured me that the perspective I'd shared was an important one for the organization to hear. I thanked them and said I would consider it, but I already knew that I didn't want to be a part of the program anymore. In fact, I stopped doing corporate presentations for many years after that, recognizing that doing so was reinforcing many of the same patterns of expression I was trying to release.

Graced by My Grandmother

That could have been the end of my Geneva story, but it wasn't. As I was walking, I suddenly realized I was ravenous. I'd passed a shawarma stand earlier and turned back to find it. Instantly, I heard a voice in my mind say, "Keep going," meaning *not* the direction of the shawarma stand.

I shrugged and smiled, thinking it was funny how much better I'd gotten at this whole intuition thing. I complied with the voice, veering away from the lake and onto the sidewalk, wondering where I'd end up and what treasures I'd find there.

After a bit of a hike, I found myself entering the edge of Old Town Geneva with its narrow cobblestone streets and alleyways. The inner voice again surprised me, "Turn left." I complied with the instruction, but as I did, it occurred to me that the voice of my intuition had never before been quite so clear and directive.

I picked up my pace, wondering if the instructions would continue and anxious to see where I was going. I soon found myself in the Bourg-de-Four Square surrounded by coffee houses, shops, and restaurants. With so many possibilities, I stopped briefly to get my bearings.

"That way," the voice insisted; I looked up across the square to the narrow street I somehow recognized as the object of the instruction.

After I'd crossed the square and began walking down that street, I became aware of two things: First, I was walking to an Orthodox Church, and second, the voice giving me directions was not my intuition, it was my *yiayia*—my mother's mother. I laughed and had to stop myself from speaking to her out loud as I walked along by myself.

"Gran! I'm going to a *church!*" Her passing had been fairly recent, and while I'd felt her presence in my space from time to time, this was different. She was actually bossing me around!

"Turn right," she told me, and I did. As I looked off down the road, I again began laughing and shaking my head in disbelief as the gold onion domes of the Cathédrale de l'Exaltation de la Sainte Croix came into my view. In cities where there was not a Greek Orthodox Church to visit, my gran would quite happily visit any Orthodox Church, and this was an absolutely stunning and architecturally significant Russian Orthodox Church. I could feel her joy buzzing in my own body, and I quickened my pace, sensing I was being presented with a rare opportunity to take my deceased grandmother somewhere she really wanted to go. In life, visiting churches to pray and venerate the icons was a devotional practice for her, a way in which she practiced gratitude.

By the time we arrived, I'd become so relaxed in her company that I actually said out loud to her, "It's closed." There was a high iron fence that marked the perimeter of the church and the gate was padlocked. As was always typical of her character, she didn't give up easily.

"Try the gate!" she directed. And even though I could see it was locked from where I was standing, I complied, rattling it to show her. Her disappointment was palpable, so I briefly looked around for a caretaker. The exterior of the church was beautiful with its Byzantine striped arches and stained-glass windows.

I felt her desire to see as much of it as possible, so I began to walk around the building, following the rectangular perimeter fence. As I arrived at what I assumed was the midpoint of the side of the church, I felt her ask me to stop and turn to face the building. When I complied, I found myself looking directly into a large white rose bush.

"Do your cross," she directed.

I hesitated. I'd always hesitated. This was a long-standing and playful "argument" between us when my gran was alive. Maybe more than anyone, she always recognized and respected that I had a strong spiritual connection. She never tried to pressure me or convince me of any specific way of believing, but she did expect me to participate in her rituals and devotionals.

In fact, she required it. Most times when I paid a visit to her and my pappou, she would fire up the charcoal in her brass censer and walk around smudging the house in frankincense and jasmine or orange. Then she would bring it over to where I was standing or sitting, waiting for me to draw the aromatic blessing of the smoke onto myself and cross myself in the Greek Orthodox tradition.

We would smile at each other, and I would always give her a sideways look like, "This time I'm not doing it."

And then she would wait patiently in front of me with smoke rising and swirling around her face until I met her in her tradition, which we both knew I was going to do.

Now, in Geneva, facing the side of the church, I could smell the fragrance of the white abundance of roses growing just inside the fence. I inhaled deeply, looked up, closed my eyes, and sent up a little prayer of gratitude for my gran's company on this day. As I bowed my head and brought my hand toward my forehead, I heard the familiar clink of her gold bangles and opened my eyes to watch in awe as, not my hand, but hers, small and brown, crossed me. Feeling an overwhelming sense of love and warmth descend upon me, I caught my breath and tears began to roll down my cheeks.

Once I regained some composure, I continued to follow the fence around the perimeter of the church, stopping at the mid-point of each of the remaining three sides to repeat this ritual with my gran.

This experience in Geneva marked a turning point for me, both professionally and personally.

Professionally, I knew I was finished with public speaking at industry conferences or workshops. In part, my confidence was singed, and I needed some time to lick my wounds and recover. But, additionally, I no longer wished to make purely intellectual or conceptual or instructional presentations. I certainly had no desire to make presentations that conformed to the steps of the scientific method.

I wanted, instead, to speak publicly about human experiences and possibilities and ideas that moved me. And I wanted to be able to bring people with me, to connect with them emotionally, and perhaps even to inspire them.

This day brought into high relief the long-standing psychic block in my ability to communicate. While I could express myself emotionally with friends and lovers one-on-one, I was still not capable of speaking the fullness of my emotional truth in groups of people. That experience stoked the fire in me to accelerate my process of learning how to show up fully when speaking in the presence of numbers of people.

The experience with my gran also brought me into a deeper, more embodied understanding of the fact that I am never alone. I am not certain exactly what it was about that time and place that made it possible for me to have such an intense sensory connection with my gran that afternoon. But since then, not a moment goes by when I am not aware that I carry with me the strengths and gifts and blessings of my grandparents and all my ancestors. I know today, more than ever, that I stand on their strong shoulders. And I offer mine to the coming generations.

Feeling and Failing

My early efforts to learn a different way were disappointing and frustrating, to say the least. I would consciously tune into my emotions and begin to sense and experience my feelings. But just as I would attempt to speak them, I could feel my intellect take over and throw me back into my head space. As this happened, the emotional resonance drained instantly out of the words, leaving only the dry descriptions, as if I were studying the feelings rather than living them.

I had taken training in public speaking myself, so I knew the techniques for varying vocal tone, using hand gestures, and making eye contact. But this wasn't about technique. In fact, as I began to attend more closely to public speaking techniques, I found some of the most powerful speakers broke all the public speaking rules and still managed to hold their audience's rapt attention.

This was about emotional connection to the audience and to the content. It felt as if they were delivering the material along with their love and devotion. In other words, their expression brought with it both the feminine-receptive and the masculine-assertive energies. The feminine brought the relatedness, the interpersonal connection with the audience, and the emotional power to the presentation. The masculine brought the structure and analytical coherence.

I was so serious about the importance of this lesson that I looked for and found a trainer in Authentic Communication. I hired her to come to the office and work with me and my team. As part of the training, we practiced telling stories that had emotional context or connection. She taught us body-centered breath techniques and physical exercises to shift our awareness and bring more emotional energy and presence into our speaking and storytelling. This work was her specialty and—though I gave it my best effort every week—over and over again I failed to stay with my emotions as I spoke. My best efforts in this 10-week program humbled and, at times, embarrassed me. I went out of my way to pick stories that were emotionally charged, hoping I might get caught up in the feelings and break the dissociative pattern.

For example, I told the story of being diagnosed with a neuromuscular disease at age 21. The diagnosis devastated me and forced a significant contraction of my life for many years. I made a point of exploring the details of the story as I presented it, how the left half of my face just stopped working, how I battled fatigue constantly, how the symptoms made me lose concentration and doubt my intelligence.

It was certainly a story rich with physical and emotional resonance, but I was not able to express it as such—even in front of this small, supportive audience of friends and coworkers. There were a few on my team, who perceived quite clearly my challenges in this regard. I can still picture one of them, shaking her head wearily as, once again, I failed to bring myself into my story completely. I simply was not in any way able to speak of the emotional pain or love or grief or joy, or any of the feelings that were so obviously a part of my life's experiences. Instead, the source of my voice remained stuck in my intellect. So I was telling stories that had the *capacity* for richness but felt dead when I told them.

The thing was, now I knew. I decided I was willing to fail as much as needed in order to learn to express myself more completely.

While I still hadn't learned how to share my emotional truth in front of a group, my efforts made me more conscious of the same dynamics in others.

I was working with a leader within a major corporation. Simon had just moved into an executive leadership role, and he wanted feedback on his communication approach. I observed him as he presented to his team of about 50 people.

He began by presenting his vision and proposed strategy. I noted as he discussed his vision and strategy that he came across as articulate, intelligent, and informed. He obviously knew what he was doing and had an excellent business rationale, but his audience was not engaged. They shuffled papers, checked emails, and shifted restlessly in their chairs. I felt the same way, coming in and out of focused attention to the details of what he was saying.

The mood reversed immediately, however, when he moved on to the topic of safety. As he began to share a story in which he had witnessed an accident on a work site that resulted in the death of a colleague, something in the essence of his communication changed.

His voice seemed to connect with his emotional center, and the air felt thick with his concern and caring. There was a palpable shift in the attention of those in the room. His entire team was now leaning slightly forward in their chairs to hear what he would say next. He went on to review a few important safety systems and processes. This material was dry, but he continued to speak from the same emotional presence that had emerged in connection with his story. And his audience stayed with him.

The capacity for expressing this combination, a balance of the emotionally present, feminine-receptive and the logical-linear, masculine-assertive was what I yearned to grow in myself.

Moving Stones

Eventually my desire to reclaim the full expression of my voice took me to Death Valley for the Vison Fast I mentioned previously, the one that brought on the dreamy post-nap visit from Kimberley's Irish ancestors. This 12-day modern rites of passage program is offered and guided by a California-based, nonprofit organization called the School of Lost Borders. The Vision Fast takes its structure and some of its basic teachings from the traditional Native American Vision Quest traditions that inspired it, but it has been adapted (lightened) to work for a wider set of participants with less awareness and experience of ceremonial practices. The guides in this organization are careful to acknowledge, honor, and respect the Native origins of their work and have received specific permissions to share certain Native American teachings in a modified context.

In this program, people come together in a natural setting to mark major life transitions, such as changes in relationship or work status and to release old ways of being that are no longer serving them. Kimberley accompanied me on this journey to support the transformation I was intending for myself.

After four days of group teachings on safety and intention, the initiates cross a threshold and hike alone to spend four days on the land fasting from food (plenty of water is taken). After four days, they return to sit in circle and tell the stories about what happened during their solo time to the guides and other fasters.

For the first four days, I sat in circle and camped in community with 10 other participants from far-flung places. I was excited to find that the program incorporated council practice, the deep communication method I'd first been taught at Naropa, as the framework for our group discussions.

We began by sharing our respective intentions with the program guides and the group. The questions we were invited to consider in shaping our intention included: "What do you want to release?" and "What gifts are you ready to step into?" When my turn came, I described my intention to release my old patterns of communication and strengthen the connection between my voice and my heart.

During the days, the guides helped us hone and refine our intentions, taught us safety and self-care techniques specific to the desert environment, and shared ancient models and body-centered practices for transformation. In the evenings, we shared meals and sat around the campfire singing songs and telling stories. These initial interactions offered yet another opportunity for me to notice my patterns. Even in this, the most accepting of communities, sitting in a circle with strangers I'd never see again, I failed again and again to speak from my emotional center.

On the morning of the fifth day, we each ventured out to our respective solo spots to spend four nights alone in nature with our intentions and to mark ceremonially our transformations in whatever ways held meaning for us.

As we crossed the threshold to leave the community base camp, the guides blessed us with a whispering of prayers, a smudging of aromatic smoke, and a brief reminder of the safety protocols. I was a hard case. I knew how to take care of myself physically, and some part of me had been craving seclusion, so I had no fear of loneliness nor of my ability to remain safe, sleeping alone under the wide desert sky.

Without realizing it, I was approaching this whole experience just as I had approached everything in my life, as if it were a physical and practical challenge. I felt proud of how I had set up my tarp and bedding and how I always stored my things in plastic bags during the days in case of rain.

At least by then I'd begun to trust my intuition, which was how I came to be in that desert in the first place. So I stayed with it; I kept listening and continued trusting. Aside from the practical instructions related to safety, I implemented none of the guides' suggestions for ceremonial practices. So there was really nothing to do. No dancing. No drumming. No speaking. No singing. For the first two days of my solo time, I sat alone and walked alone, listening to the way the desert met my heartbeat and my footsteps. Following the guidance of the small voice inside me, I wandered, sat, and slept, making occasional notes in my journal about my thoughts and movements, about the birds I saw, the winding trees trailing strings of bark, and the astonishing aliveness of the desert. On the third day, I began walking west from my solo sleeping spot.

About midday, in need of a rest, I lay down on a large flat rock and allowed the sun to warm me. After some time, I sat up to get my bearings and decided to continue my walk, rather than turning back. As I sat there, a small stone flashing in the sun caught my eye, so I leaned forward, picked it up, and turned it over in my hand. It was pure white and worn completely smooth but otherwise quite unremarkable. Feeling a sort of reverence for the desert that had been emerging in me during my solo time, I carefully placed the stone back where I'd found it and rose to leave.

After taking a few steps down the path, I had the impression the little white stone was calling me. And not in an ambiguous way. I mean, I kind of heard it yelling, "Hey! Hey! You forgot me! Take me with you!"

Remembering that the guides had encouraged us to pay close attention and listen for messages in nature, I shrugged and returned to retrieve the stone hitchhiker. As I pocketed it, I chuckled, musing to myself, "Maybe I'm crazy, but at least I'm a good listener."

Feeling drawn farther west toward a large dark geologic feature rising from the muted dusty desert, I continued walking. When I reached it, I scrambled to the top, expecting that from that elevated vista I might see at least one of my fellow fasters. Not a soul in sight, but I did realize that I was now standing on a volcanic formation with lots of interesting outcroppings, crannies, and irregularities that were worth exploring. Energized, I walked gingerly around the top of the formation looking for a good place to descend and investigate further. Finding my way down to the ground on the far side, I followed the perimeter, feeling in and out of the dark, serpentine cragginess.

As I made my way, I began to feel a strange kind of anticipation, and my mind flashed to the stone in my pocket. Rounding a sharp corner, I stopped abruptly to take in more fully what I was seeing. I had discovered the entrance to what seemed like a natural cathedral carved out of the black volcanic rock. With a height from floor to ceiling of maybe 15 feet, it wasn't as large as a traditional cathedral, but its shape and majesty inspired a similar feeling in me. The crunching sound of my steps reverberated as I stepped carefully across the oval floor. The walls sloped up and inward to a wide opening at the ceiling, through which the bluest slice of sky was visible, and large shafts of sunlight beamed in. Just off center from the middle, a natural structure in the same black rock jutted up from the ground. Walking around it, I noticed it had formed naturally into the shape of an altar, with a flat shelf at the level of my shoulders and a backdrop shaped something like a rounded shrine.

I was still marveling at the beauty of this discovery when I was surprised by a small voice calling to me from my pocket, "Here!

This is it! This is where I go!" I laughed to myself and shook my head, reaching into my pocket for my little hitchhiker stone. By then, I'd become quite attached to it and was hoping to take it home with me. I held it momentarily in the palm of my hand and again looked closely at it.

"What? Here?" I asked it, gesturing to the altar, although I already knew the answer.

It was the right thing to do, but I felt strangely protective thinking of leaving that tiny white stone in the midst of all that volcanic darkness. It seemed a brave and futile request, but I complied. I briefly cupped it in my hands, drew it to my chest, then bowed my head and placed the stone carefully in the center of the altar. Stepping back with my hands on my heart, I looked up from the entrance to see the stone in its place and was immediately overcome with emotion and gratitude.

After four days of solo time, I returned to base camp, with a hunger for food and connection and a wobbly uncertainty. Had my time been well spent? Would anything change at all? Was I even willing to share the crazy-sounding story of the encounter with the white stone I'd befriended?

Circling Stories

After a celebratory meal and a good night's sleep, I met the guides and my fellow fasters back in our council circle. The process from here was for each participant to tell the story of what transpired during our solo time, to share what happened for us when we took our intentions out onto the land.

The storytelling process is, for many, the most powerful part of the ceremony. One by one, each faster tells the story of their time away—the animals they encountered, the way they constructed their shelter, their responses to the weather and other challenges, the walks they took, the songs they sang, etc. No two stories are ever remotely similar.

After each faster's story, the guides reflect back, or "mirror," the story, helping the faster to more completely integrate and recognize the unconscious guidance present in the story itself.

The guides explained that the purpose of mirroring in this context is to "empower the story." They listened deeply while each story was being told, and then each guide took a turn repeating certain aspects of the story back to the faster with great reverence and emotional intensity, inserting occasional props and humor.

In the retelling, they emphasized the storyteller-faster's intention and feelings, even sometimes drawing out connections in the story to universal archetypes, symbols, and myths.

With the telling and mirroring of each faster's story, I sensed the level of trust, connection, and communion of the group grow deeper, the walls between us gradually disintegrating. We laughed and wept together openly with everyone's joys and griefs and discoveries. There is a way in which this kind of storytelling and mirroring speaks to something ancient in us and moves us emotionally in ways that the hard facts of science do not and are not intended to approach. The practice touches a deep need of the psyche to connect through stories and to learn through symbols and metaphors.

Had I ever, I wondered, listened to someone's story with this level of attention? Had anyone ever listened to me this deeply? If I had to point to a single aspect of this intense 12-day experience as most powerful for me, it would be witnessing and feeling the impact of the telling and mirroring of stories. This process had fostered an almost immediate connection among people with diverse cultural backgrounds and life experiences. I'd found myself dropping into uncommon depths of emotional intimacy with a group of people I'd known for less than two weeks.

When my turn came to share the story of my own solo time, I felt at ease, knowing my new community of friends would listen with compassion and reverence.

So I spoke spontaneously without censoring. I explained how I didn't feel drawn to any of the structures, practices, or recommendations the guides had offered during our preparations. I told them about how I'd set up my sleep spot and about my daily walks. I talked about the notes I'd made in my journal, including the scribbled rant about how very tired I was of myself and whatever it was inside me that continued to derail me and prevent me from speaking the truth of my feelings.

Finally, in some detail, I related my encounter with the little hitchhiker stone, how I'd carried it with me on my walk westward and imagined I would bring it home with me. I told of my climb up the volcanic feature and my discovery of the black cathedral with its natural altar formation. And then, in a whisper of tears full of tenderness and gratitude, I told them of the white stone's request to be placed upon the altar and left there. In that instant, I felt it. Something had shifted and I had—at least for a moment—spoken my heart's truth to this group.

Out of Balance: Individuality and Independence

The trends are alarming. Our national suicide rate is at a 30-year high. Substance abuse, particularly of opiates, has become epidemic. Mental illness has become the second most common cause of disability in the US.[7]

---

7 Kirsten Weir, "Worrying Trends in U.S. Suicide Rates," American Psychological Association, March 2019, https://www.apa.org/monitor/2019/03/trends-suicide.

Despite our relative prosperity, the trends indicate that Americans are increasingly depressed and anxious and looking for ways to escape these feelings. We are obsessed with the newest distractions and applications available on our ever-present smartphones. We spend hours entertaining ourselves, following our favorites on social media, and broadcasting our grievances with the finale of our preferred Netflix series. We stream our music and podcasts to keep any silence at bay.

Our cultural and systemic biases toward the masculine-assertive expression teach us to see ourselves primarily as individuals—separate and complete and wholly responsible for our own independent journey. The pervasiveness of this perspective makes it challenging for us to know and value ourselves as a meaningful part of the interdependent web of life on the planet…but we know it anyway. We sense intrinsically that we are fundamentally and inextricably connected to all other life on earth.

To some degree, we feel the pain of those among us whose needs and illnesses are left untended. We feel in our hearts and bodies the grief of the losses of our forests and the pollution of our waterways.

We reinforce the myth of our separation by insulating ourselves more and more from an awareness of our connection to the natural world. Many of us live in larger homes than we grew up in and we've accumulated around us a cushion of vastly more possessions than we need to sustain us.

We carefully control the range of light and temperature in our environments, minimizing our awareness of the earth's seasons and natural cycles. Our GPS applications have relieved us of the need to attend to environmental landmarks and the movement of the sun to find our way. And the ever-present thrum of advertising in our midst continues to tell us we will be happier with the comfort afforded by one more convenience device or luxury product.

Overwhelmed with the busyness of all our doing, many with the means to do so hire help with the lawn care and landscaping, so we are less likely to experience the sensation of dirt under our fingernails or the magic of an emerging seedling.

Regardless of the time of year, we can buy almost every kind of fruit and vegetable, leaving us with no awareness of what food grows in our local ecosystems and during which seasons. Our garbage is hauled off to places we will likely never visit, so we are insulated from the experience of knowing its impact directly.

Even though we already have the science necessary to demonstrate the effects of our overconsumption of natural resources and the associated environmental degradation, all we really need to recognize the significance of our impact is our full attention.[8]

We are surrounded by the evidence. It's in our dumpsters and in our rivers. It's visible in our air and on our ocean floors. It's observable in the clearcutting of forests and the destruction of habitat for many species of animals. And because it is the truth of our nature that we are interdependent with all life on this planet, we intuitively *feel and know and respond* to these things. Consciously or unconsciously, we feel the effects.

We feel them emotionally as grief from the losses of life in all its forms and as the pain of our alienation from the natural world, which we know intrinsically to be both our home and our body. We sense the effects, physically, as a visceral yearning for our disappearing wild spaces and in our instinctive wince upon first sight of a bulldozer in a treasured green space. We know the positive side of this emotional connection as our love for our pets and delight in our gardens.

---

8   Mark Sagoff, "Do We Consume Too Much?," The Atlantic (Atlantic Media Company, September 26, 2014), https://www.theatlantic.com/magazine/archive/1997/06/do-we-consume-toomuch/376877/.

We are regularly presented with opportunities to become more sensitive to the effects of our activities on all of life and to our sweet earth, herself a living organism. Connecting more fully to our own emotional and physical responses in connection with our actions will awaken us to the deep wisdom of our own feminine-receptive aspect and will inform us of the ways to best serve the great web of life.

Does our collective estrangement from the other half of our full human expression represent a source of the pain that so many are attempting to escape or anesthetize? What broader wisdom and truth of our human existence have we forgotten? What healing might be available to us if we allow ourselves consciously to reconnect with nature and with life, to be mindful and to turn toward these aspects of ourselves and the feelings associated with them, whether joy or grief, aversion or gratitude?

Practices:
Connection and Mindfulness

It's increasingly rare for us to be present for the miracle of a green sprouting seedling. We are literally inspired and fed by the presence of new growth in our midst. And devoting ourselves to the tending of another living thing connects us to the—sometimes forgotten—essential qualities of tenderness and compassion inherent to our human experience and expression.

Grow something from a seed. Start small. Plant a single flower, herb, or vegetable in a pot, and nurture it into full growth. Over time, as the plant grows, allow yourself to begin to sense what it needs. Less water? More light? Move it to a different room or location from time to time. Notice the difference it makes in your experience of the various rooms of your home. Observe any changes or reactions, both in the plant and in you. Consider documenting your observances and feelings in a journal or sketch pad.

In the swirl of our busy lives, the effort associated with meal planning, preparation, and clean up can feel overwhelming to us. We can easily fall into the habit of eating pre-prepared meals or grabbing take out. There is, however, something essential that happens when we attend to the preparation of our tables with mindfulness and devotion; it's a form of magic making. Our most ancient myths are full of stories of the blessings that come to those who intentionally set a table and lovingly prepare a nourishing meal for those in their midst.

Plan, prepare, and serve a meal with the fullness of your attention and devotion. Consider a family recipe that you love or one that connects to your ancestry. Ask for help with the other things on your to-do list so you can focus on the meal exclusively. Make your shopping list and savor the sensory process of selecting every ingredient. As you prepare the dinner, consider singing or saying a blessing over it at every stage of the process. Allow yourself to imagine your family and/or dinner guests enjoying and being nourished by it. Set the table mindfully with fresh flowers or greenery and your nicest place settings. Light candles, seat your guests, and consider sharing a blessing, a reading, a poem, or a memory before inviting everyone to begin eating together.

Post-dinner, guests clean up while the cook relaxes.

Most of us never really get to see a wild space that is anywhere near its natural state. The minute we arrive, the animals scatter. We make noise without thinking, and we step on growing things without noticing. We commonly think of hikes in the woods as exercise goals, missing out on the opportunity for real communion with nature.

Visit the woods or another wild space. Leave your phone in the car, and enter the woods as quietly and unobtrusively as possible. Sit under a tree—or even in a tree—for 30 minutes, and observe what lives and what happens around you. Tune into your senses. Notice any changes in your state of mind. Walk silently and mindfully to a different location and repeat, taking notice of the differences in the inner and outer landscapes.

The miracle of digital technology has transformed our lives. We have instant access to all sorts of information in a myriad of formats, we are constantly bombarded with advertisements, and our attention is diverted by the buzzes and beeps of notifications from our mobile apps. We no longer have to wait until prime time to watch our favorite shows, and we have the ability to communicate with each other seamlessly over thousands of miles. While these technologies have enriched our lives in many ways, they also remove us from a receptivity to what's happening in our physical proximity in the current moment.

Practice presence. Take a breather from the miracle and stay off all digital technology, including your personal electronic devices. Refrain from using your smartphone or computer for 24 hours. Use this break from your favorite electronics to open your senses to the sights, sounds, and other physical sensations of the world that exists around you. Hold the intention to take in and be informed by your surroundings. Make note of any insights from this experience.

We have become accustomed to separating ourselves from the natural world, especially at night when our vision is limited. We stay indoors, insulated and removed from any awareness of the changes in the natural light and the weather. The night sky is reduced to a beautiful backdrop we appreciate through our closed windows.

Take your sleeping bag to a campsite, your balcony, or your back yard, and sleep outdoors with no walls, no roof, and no electronics. Make yourself as comfortable as possible (suffering is not the point), and nestle yourself down under the stars. Control your own temperature with clothing and bedding choices. Notice the sounds and animals and images that emerge in the darkness. Tune in to the changes in temperature and the sky throughout the night.

In time, as you experiment with one or more of these practices, you will begin to sense an opening that strengthens your connection to the feminine-receptive and reminds you of some of what you might have forgotten as you've taken on the out-of-balance expectations of our culture. I hope you feel energized by the possibilities and inspired to find ways to create more balance in your own expression in this life.

CHAPTER 5

No Control Group

When Hope Is a Plan

There have not been many moments in my adult life when I have been physically overcome by joy and enthusiasm. I learned well to remain anchored in issues of the practical. That didn't leave much space for art, either the expression of it or the appreciation of it.

So I was completely taken by surprise when I caught myself literally jumping up and down, whooping, and slapping my hands on the dresser while I first heard the story of "Store Buyout." It goes like this: a group of four gutsy young performance artists get together and decide to buy out a store.

"I mean, think about it," said Kyle, the originator of the idea, to the group. "They're asking for it...all those shelves chock full of stuff...and no one ever actually comes in and says, 'I'll take it all!'"

Even though this crew of artists had no real source of funding and no idea how exactly to make it happen, they all nodded their heads meaningfully with a real appreciation for the potential of the idea and responded to this inspiration with a wholehearted, "Yes." In fact, they all agreed to meet in New York and find a way to buy out a store.

Just a few weeks later in New York City, the group visited Hercules Fancy Grocery, a quirky little neighborhood corner store with a locally famous cat named Sneaky and a great selection of imported beers. Hercules was about to lose his lease; the combination of high downtown rents and the extended economic downturn had finally taken its toll, and he was being forced to close up shop.

Hercules is a soft-spoken man with a thick Greek accent and a sweet smile. He had been running grocery stores in New York for 40 years. The four artists agreed on the spot that this is the store they will buy out, and they will do it as a surprise to Hercules. They had less than two weeks to figure out where to get the money, what to do with all the stuff after they bought it, and how to transport it from the store to an as yet unidentified storage location.

As I have found is often the case for certain creative types, they pulled together about 50 percent of the plan and trusted the rest would work itself out. Within a few days, the team walked in with a briefcase containing $10,000 in cash and bought out Hercules Fancy Grocery. One item at a time, they emptied every shelf as Hercules tracked the total on his adding machine. It took most of a day but they did it; they removed every last thing from the store— from beer and ice cream sandwiches to toilet paper and chewing gum—and loaded it all into a rental van illegally parked out front. Once they had paid Hercules for their purchases, this crew of artists transported everything to borrowed space in a warehouse where they celebrated success and brainstormed next steps with friends, ice cream, and imported beers. What did they do with all the stuff they bought? They reimagined these common items as works of art, of course. And then they listed them for sale on the internet.

Just a few weeks later, I found myself poring over the details of this story online, watching and rewatching the videos compiled during the events and being moved to tears by the whole thing.

It took me a little time to fully understand what exactly it was about the Store Buyout story that so touched and delighted me. While, in the end, this production didn't save Hercules' store, it did serve to help him clear out all his inventory and go out with a bang. It gave everyone, Hercules included, an amazing experience as well.

While the videos have a quality of madcap fun to them, they also documented a few moments of pure human connection. In one segment, Hercules' voice cracks with emotion as he tells one of the artists about how much gratitude he feels for his customers. When asked about his wishes for the future, he said he wished happiness to the Store Buyout artists and their families.

The videos of Hercules touched me in a deeply familiar way; his tender demeanor and his accent reminded me of my Greek-Cypriot grandfather, my pappou.

Perhaps what most amazed and moved me about the Store Buyout story was the receptivity of the other three artists to Kyle's big, irrational, artistic impulse. No one among them suggested the idea was impossible, or even unlikely. No one said it was stupid. No one did anything to imply it was an undertaking unworthy of consideration. *No one said, "No."* I strained even to imagine such a scenario. But it went even further than that. *They all said, "Yes."*

Not only were Kyle's cohorts receptive to the idea, they each agreed to add their energy. It's important to note that there was originally no altruistic objective associated with the Store Buyout concept; there was only a creative seed, a possibility that wasn't snuffed out. In fact, it was the initial, receptive "yes" that created the conditions for that creative seed to germinate and grow into a full-on act of kindness and connection.

What would it be like, I wondered, to be surrounded by people who recognized and said "yes" to inspired, creative ideas? What would it be like, I wondered, if *I* were a person who recognized and said "yes" to inspired, creative ideas?

I'd made myself late to work trying to wrap my head around this story and was sitting there on the bed dumbfounded. I felt a strong yearning somehow to participate, to extend this art movement, to somehow say "yes" to it myself.

"Yes" adds energy to thoughts, ideas, and actions; it keeps possibilities open. I clicked the link to the Store Buyout website, where the artists had posted for sale a selection of the art they'd created from the products they'd purchased. I lost even more time there, delighting at the humorous naming and artistic packaging of ordinary grocery story items in plexiglass display cases—a Bic lighter was listed as "Portable Sun," and there were listings for a "Very Rare Upside-Down Coke" (i.e., an upside-down Coke) and a "Human Battery" (two Red Bulls, one upright and one inverted). But I felt my heart skip a beat when I saw the listing for the cruddy plastic briefcase that was used to carry the cash into the store for the purchases. The price for the briefcase was listed at $10,000. But here's the kicker: according to the listing, the artists themselves would personally travel to deliver the briefcase to the purchaser and would, while there, participate in an event in the city of the purchaser.

I heard myself whisper, "I want to buy that briefcase." I must've whispered more loudly than I thought because Kimberley's head popped out of the closet.

Eyes wide, she said, "Oh my God! I was thinking the same thing! I want to buy that briefcase!"

Through much laughter and disbelief, we found a way to purchase that $10,000 briefcase. It took us about half a day to convince PayPal that we really wanted them to process this transaction on our credit cards.

And over the following few days, we checked in with each other a couple of times a day, "How you doing? Still feel okay about the briefcase?"

"Oh yeah…might be my favorite purchase ever. You?"

"Yep! Glorious."

Years later, I can say without hesitation it's still one of my favorite investments.

Over the years, I have told the story of Store Buyout and our purchase of the briefcase many times. Some people get it immediately. Others nod slowly like they are waiting for the end of the story, the punchline, where we get all the money back and this whole thing makes sense. In case your reaction falls in the latter category, let me go ahead and close that loop.

We never got the money back. We were nowhere near independently wealthy, and we had no more of a plan when we agreed to buy the briefcase than did the four artists when they agreed to meet in New York to buy out a store. We had no idea what type of event we might have…no idea of when, where, or whom we might invite. We just recognized intuitively that buying that briefcase was the right next step for us. And we trusted the rest of the plan would eventually work itself out.

This kind of knowing and trusting has become more routine for me as I have learned to value and hold space for my own receptivity and intuition. I recognize true inspiration because I feel it; it feels like a "yes" in my body and soul. This intuitive knowing is the energy of the feminine-receptive.

In this case, that inspired, intuitive "yes" was ultimately energized by the masculine-assertive action of the briefcase purchase. This combination of inspiration—received and recognized by the feminine aspect—and manifestation—embodied and actioned by the masculine aspect—is how the divine balance of the inspired creative expresses itself through us.

Dancing with Yes

For the culminating event, we invited the city of Houston, Texas, to dance through the streets with us. We teamed up with the Store Buyout artists to organize and crowdfund a Decentralized Dance Party. A Decentralized Dance Party, or DDP, is an all-night roving street dance powered by social media and boom boxes; it was the invention, passion, and occupation of Gary Lachance, one of the Store Buyout artists. Gary rigged up a system that allows him to broadcast the same party mix to hundreds of boom boxes at the same time. These boom boxes are carried through the streets by the hundreds (and sometimes thousands) of partygoers who show up at the appointed time and place. Gary's been taking the DDP to the streets in different cities since 2009, and his intention is clear and consistent: "Unite people through a night of Capital P Partying."

He is very serious about it. On his website, he describes the experience:

Participants become performers and inhibitions are overwhelmed as we all rise together in a chaotic and joyful monument to the Human Spirit. Together, we awaken the raw and beautiful rhythm and adventure-craving instincts ingrained in our DNA that have been subverted since childhood in our sterile western cultures....

Consistently, participants describe the DDP experience as the best night of their lives.

After the Houston DDP, I documented a few of the most mind-bending moments in my journal:

Snapshot 1

The party is in motion underneath an overpass, and Gary calmly invites the crowd to form a dance circle. Encouraged by dancers dressed as bananas, the crowd complies, and an impossibly diverse series of people makes their way to the center of the circle dancing wildly in ones and twos amidst peals of laughter and appreciative whooping from the crowd. A dance battle spontaneously breaks out between a young woman dressed in a T-Rex costume and another young woman dressed as a panda. The two completely enjoy the drama of this moment, grimacing fiercely and taking turns throwing down wicked dance moves

This is WTF territory on so many levels with squeals and tears of bent-over laughter in the crowd. There's just no frame of reference for processing such ridiculousness. Somehow between the laughing and dancing, my thoughts go from, "Are we actually dancing in a circle underneath an overpass in downtown Houston?" to "How did they decide to wear those costumes?" to "No, really. Am I dancing in the street with bananas, a T-Rex, and a panda?" Perhaps, there is an in-the-moment-ness, a kind of ecstatic presence, which can only be brought around by the simultaneous experience of so many layers of outrageous improbability. I will never forget the incredulous joy in the faces of the people in that circle.

Snapshot 2

The party crowd dance-treks through the park at Discovery Green, picking up a few more people along the way. Like kids at a wedding, we disco, spin, and hop up onto the dimly lit empty stage next to the ice rink. After a few fast-paced tunes, including a dedication to the late-night Zamboni driver ("YMCA" by the Village People), Gary cues up a slow song: "I Don't Want to Miss a Thing" by Aerosmith. As this song plays, the crowd goes from twirling and swaying alone or in pairs to a large group-hug mass slow dancing and singing in a collective embrace. I was hugging the outside perimeter of the mosh with friends, when a Hawaiian-shirted man, a couple of layers in, motioned for us to come in closer. We squeezed in and held on tighter. We'd begun the dance as 150 people—mostly strangers to each other, various ages, multiple races, people in banana costumes, people in club wear, people who planned to be there, and people we picked up on the way—and we ended it as a single, breathing unit. No one wanted that song to end.

Snapshot 3

A crowd of people carrying vintage boom boxes, some dressed as bananas, dance through a manicured downtown park and rapidly surround the perimeter of a sunken basketball court. On the court below, a dozen or so bewildered kids and adults take notice and stop their play. Smiles slowly break across their faces and some laugh and begin to bounce to the base-heavy dubstep music blaring from the synchronized boom boxes. The DDP crowd files down the stairs and begins to cheer as the kids take turns shooting three-pointers. A couple of the bananas confer and agree that one of the more spherical boom boxes should be substituted for a basketball in a series of dunking and free throw experiments. Basketballers and partygoers erupt in laughter at the absurdity as the boom box is repeatedly sent aloft from the free throw line. Eventually, we all end up on the court, dancing "the wobble." I had the feeling I'd been dropped into a heartwarming movie scene I would have criticized for not being realistic.

Snapshot 4

After four hours of dance partying through downtown Hous-

ton, the DDP winds up in a parking lot next to a high-rise building around 1:00 am. Before cueing up the final song of the night, Gary instructs the group to line up all the boom boxes on the ground in the corner of the parking lot. Exhausted, but not ready to leave, the grateful crowd begins swaying arm-in-arm to the marathon ballad, "I'd Do Anything for Love (but I Won't Do That)" by Meatloaf. We suddenly become aware of a competing tune nearby: "Turkey in the Straw," and an ice cream truck—speaker blaring—bumps over the ramp and up into the parking lot. Incredulous laughter and delighted whoops ensue as partiers load up on water and ice cream bars. Gary restarts the song, and I notice some people are looking up, reaching to the sky, singing and swaying. Following the direction of their gaze, I see the silhouette of a woman in a window about 20 stories up. She has her arms up against the window and is swaying and dancing with the crowd on the ground. The whole DDP group joins in and finishes this last dance with the window woman.

The Houston DDP both was and was not a party. I mean, there was music and dancing and revelry, but it was nothing like any party I'd ever attended.

The experience changed me. I felt as if we'd all collectively stepped across a threshold, gone through some kind of portal, and embarked on an ecstatic journey to an alternate, unified universe. Over the course of the evening, we skipped and twirled and ran through fountains like children, we laughed and cried and sang together, and we embraced and remembered ourselves as the long-lost family we are.

I have come to believe that, in his design of the DDP, Gary intuitively recreated an ancient model for group communion and creative expression that has been mostly forgotten by western culture. Indigenous cultures around the world have known and employed similar models for millennia.

The DDP establishes a context in which large, diverse groups of people feel safe to step out of their ordinary patterns of movement and interaction and experiment with new possibilities.

Gary moderates the energy of the crowd by changing the music track, moving to the next location on the party route, and providing gentle but firm guidance when necessary to maintain the physical and emotional safety of the group. The bananas play an important role as well, modeling the way by dancing with abandon and engaging playfully and spontaneously with people, props, and the physical environment.

Over the course of the evening, as the collective trust builds, partygoers continue to drop their inhibitions and move more freely still. Perhaps for the first time since childhood, participants experience themselves and others moving and interacting in a shared creative field of spontaneity and joy.

The foundational structure of the DDP is an expression of the masculine-assertive, with its consistent preparatory steps, clear instructions, and intentional route design. However, the structure is flexible and open enough to allow and invite the flow of inspiration and intuition of the feminine-receptive. It is this combination that allows for the emergence of spontaneous, creative movement and engagement. And creative collective movement and engagement are, incidentally, the dynamics most needed to address the world's most pressing problems.

The artists used the $10,000 to travel to us in Houston and to help pay off the debt of the products they purchased themselves, as well as for other art projects.

For me, the event was transformative in large part because it taught me the power of saying "yes." When we allow ourselves to say "yes" to the tingling feeling of inspiration knocking at the door or our hearts, we open ourselves to joy and new discoveries that we will miss if we always force ourselves back to the desk and the dishes. Certainly, discipline and planning have their place, but not everything requires a map or a plan.

Since I have come to this realization, I am more likely to pause at an invitation and ask myself, "Is there a way I can say 'yes' to this?" And if I can, I do. Not all of my yeses turn into magic dances with thrilling outcomes. But all my favorite stories and my greatest life adventures all began with me saying "yes" to the right next step according to my fluttery heart's knowing.

Experiments in Face-Planting

I first heard a description of the Bound Lotus Kriya (Baddha Padmasana) during one of the weekend classes in my yoga teacher training program.

Hari Kirn, the petite, funny wife of Sat Kartar—both teachers in my yoga teacher training—described it thusly, "Well, first you come into Full Lotus seated position with your feet placed here at the very top of your thighs, and then you reach your arms around behind your back crossing them, bring your hands forward to grab your big toes, bend forward, and rest your head on the floor in front of you."

I remember laughing out loud and shaking my head, thinking, "Holy crap, *rest* your head! Really? Here's one more thing on the long list of things I am never, ever going to do." I just knew it was out of the question. I had always been physically strong, but I'd never been particularly flexible. "I'll find other postures," I thought, "I'll do other sets."

Although Bound Lotus seemed unattainable when Hari Kirn first described it, something in me knew, even then, that this kriya held a certain personal significance. My decision to work with it evolved over the next several years, beginning with a strange sort of intuition that flashed into my consciousness on a fairly regular basis, unbidden and apropos of nothing: "Now would be good to put your head on the ground."

In my thirties I would never have been aware of such an impulse. I was mostly out of touch with the wisdom of my body back then and far too focused on my practical plans for the day. It was only after 10 years of body awareness work, including yoga, dance, fasting, and other somatic consciousness practices that I came to recognize and attend to intuitive physical yearnings like this.

And so it was, after a couple of particularly difficult professional setbacks, I became aware of the oddly consistent physical yearning to put my head on the ground.

I started experimenting with putting my head on the ground when no one was looking—just to see how it felt. I tried it indoors and outdoors. And I don't mean just to lie down comfortably with my cheek on the ground—I mean, face down. I occasionally burst out laughing, imagining how ridiculous I looked, lying face down in the grass. But I kept trying anyway. I changed my daily morning meditation practice—incorporating time on my knees with my forehead on the ground. I experimented with the sensation of bowing movements, over and over, bringing my head to the ground.

It had been years since I had heard Hari Kirn describe the kriya, "...and rest your head on the ground..." but I thought of her again, and after a quick search, I found a website with detailed instructions and modifications for working with Bound Lotus Kriya. I have been regularly practicing this kriya ever since.

Only once or twice during my years of practice have I been able to find my way completely into this challenging posture, but what

I have gained from the experience of working with Bound Lotus has made the perfection of the posture itself seem secondary to me (okay, almost secondary).

For example, when I decided to practice this kriya, I decided I would also practice active self-compassion; I knew I was going to be bad at this posture for a while—possibly forever—so I decided I was only ever going to be kind to myself about it. Learning to hold this kind of compassion for myself opened me to a greater compassion for the individual and collective efforts of others.

My years of working with Bound Lotus have been full of life lessons. Some days, I find myself unable even to get my legs into the Full Lotus position, and I adapt the practice because pain is not the point.

Other days, inexplicably, the lotus position feels wonderful in my body, my head drops to the floor without strain or hesitation and I can just about grab both toes.

Certain days, I feel annoyed by the practice from beginning to end. Other days, I feel immense gratitude and peace throughout. In these ways, the regular practice of showing up to this challenge reminds me over and over that my expression is variable and that it matters at least as much that I bring myself consistently and with curiosity to my life experiences as it does how well I perform the task at hand.

Symbolically, holding myself in this immobile position with my head on the ground is the most tangible, least subtle way I could possibly be reminded to "stay grounded," "surrender," and "allow," which are all expressions of the feminine-receptive aspect.

People tend to think of yoga as a practice that builds physical flexibility. But physical flexibility is only one aspect of what we learn through the practice of moving our bodies differently, whether in yoga, dance, a Couch to 5K program, or a different body-centered practice. Moving differently systematically creates and strengthens new neural pathways in the brain and nervous system, which in turn create flexibility in how we think and move in the world.

So while stillness and surrender can be a challenge for those of us taught to value movement and action and making things happen, learning to embody it has opened me to a much richer and more expansive experience of my life. If we can learn to surrender, we can begin to create openings and possibilities that allow us to express more balance in our lives.

CHAPTER 6

Going to School on the Feminine

Lime and Elbow Grease

"I'm going to be using an ancient plastering process in there," my friend Sara told me, pointing to the unusable shower in mid-remodel.

"Oh," I replied, "and when are you planning to have it done?"

"I have no idea," she replied through a wry smile, "It takes a long time to do...it involves lots of layers of lime and elbow grease. I have never done it before, and the process involves hand polishing and compacting the lime into a stone-like surface."

Confused, I asked her if she was considering hiring someone else do to the work. She told me she felt it was important for her to do it herself, that there is a way in which her hands-on engagement creates a certain kind of sacred and soulful connection with her home.

Intrigued by this perspective, I continued with my questions, "So...like, are we talking weeks? Months?"

She turned to look at me, seemingly amused by my singular focus on completion and replied simply, "Could be."

I was mystified by these answers and at the same time my curiosity was piqued.

Sara is known in the community as a gifted designer of home spaces, specializing in helping her clients select colors and make other decisions about the composition of their living spaces. But that description is not how she sees her work.

She describes it as a cocreation of "sacred sanctuary," and she told me that the work she does is largely intuitive and relational. She also explained that it can be particularly challenging to work in this way when business models are so focused on end goals, deadlines, and plans. While people often hire her because they want her to replicate a home design she did for a different client, she says intuitively she recognizes that what they are really looking for is a certain kind of experience, the experience of sanctuary.

Sara has taught me a lot about the feminine-receptive expression as it relates to how we respond to the spaces we inhabit. She is tremendously sensitive to the effects of space, color, and materiality and has developed a mastery of the ways in which our environments impact us on both individual and collective levels.

Her teachings on this topic were never linear, weaving in and out of descriptions of process, space, color, emotional response, materiality, beauty, and the significance of soulful, hands-on creation.

The experience of sanctuary, she told me, can only be cocreated with her clients because the balance and selection of design elements are unique to each person; they are drawn from our individual internal maps and associations, based on our own sensitivities, emotional responses, habits, and needs.

So whether her clients are more or less aware of the process, most of the initial work she does with them is an intuitive and receptive process in which she comes to understand, with their input, the combinations of colors, materials, and space arrangements that most closely reflect those internal maps and that will best serve their particular experiences of beauty and sanctuary.

There are, Sara taught me, some universal truths that contribute more generally to an experience of sanctuary. For example, whether or not we are consciously aware of it, we all have the ability to perceive whether or not our buildings and the items we keep inside of them were artfully and soulfully created.

"If something is made by hand with love, at whatever scale…a building, a planter, a necklace, anything…," Sara told me, "it's as if the beauty of that inspiration is always present in that thing, and it will be felt and experienced consciously or unconsciously by those who encounter it through time."

She went on to explain that environments and items that are made of more natural and non-processed materials will be more likely to align with and convey a felt sense of beauty and sanctuary.

Sara's teachings helped me to attend more mindfully to the combination of emotions and physical sensations I have as I move through different environments and interact with materials, furnishings, and other items in those environments.

I have, hanging in my living room, a composition of the icon of Saint Barbara. The piece once belonged to my grandparents and hung over the bed in their village home on the island of Cyprus.

I don't know the detailed story of its creation, but it appears that the image of the saint was originally printed on a piece of fabric and then hand varnished, slightly off center, onto a piece of wood. The frame is obviously handmade and at some point, it was painted a brick red color along with the border around the print. In certain places, there are wayward red brush marks where the painter overlapped the edges of the print.

While the construction is imperfect and this piece is in no way valuable in a monetary sense, it is one of my most treasured possessions. I sense a soulfulness in it perhaps related in some degree to the reverence and devotion that inspired its original creation. I also sense from it the spiritual connection it held for my grandparents and later for my mother, who gifted it to me.

Because our economic system is overbalanced toward the masculine-assertive aspect, with a focus on mass production and growth, we have developed efficient manufacturing and distribution systems that make wide varieties of consumer and convenience goods immediately available and accessible in many parts of the world. And there are ways in which these goods can be seen to have improved the standard of living for many.

But if we compare these items, manufactured and mass produced by robots in automated factories, with those produced by the skilled and loving hand of a craftsperson or artist, we immediately sense the difference.

We feel the difference between a wool rug woven by a skilled Navajo weaver and an acrylic machine-made imitation. It's the feminine-receptive aspect that feels and perceives, that knows in the body and spirit, this difference.

When we become more aware of these differences, we are better able to understand what we most need in our environments to feel nourished and inspired. We can begin to bring a different kind of attention and curiosity to our environments, asking questions like, "What is it about this room that feels so relaxing and homey?" "How do the colors of that rug feel to me?" "Why am I not moved by that photograph?" Or even, "Why does this building always seem to sap my energy?"

Since I started paying closer attention to the construction and configuration of spaces as well as the furnishings, art, and other items held within those spaces, I am better able to create beautiful and nurturing living and working environments for myself and to help others do the same. This process requires that we engage with the feminine-receptive, that we take in, feel, and sense the impacts that spaces and colors and shapes and creations have on us.

We are always in a relationship with the spaces we inhabit. The best living and working spaces remind us of who we are and nurture us at a soul level. And, in turn, we engage the masculine-assertive aspect to nurture those environments back by loving and caring for the buildings and spaces along with the items, activities, and people within them.

Touched by Twombly

The exterior design of the Cy Twombly Gallery in Houston is simple and modern. With subtle signage and an entrance not visible from the street, it's easy to miss.

By the time I stepped inside, my hands were already trembling. I had caught sight of the rough-thrown sculpture in the entry and the looping scribbles in the far room, and I was having some sort of visceral response.

I stopped for a moment to catch my breath and check myself. I had experienced something a bit like this walking through the Van Gogh museum in Amsterdam a few years ago, but this reaction was more immediate and intense. I lost time wandering through the various rooms and arrangements of Twombly's paintings and sculptures, allowing these emotional and physical responses to ebb and flow within me.

One of the largest rooms is entirely dedicated to a single painting, the visual story of which takes up a long wall. In irregularly shaped mixes of yellows and reds and blues that reach all the way up the wall, the visual story culminates with a descending flow of similar shapes in deeper reds and yellows, obscured in part by concentrations of the darkest blues and blacks.

I sat down on the bench opposite and alternated between looking at the work and putting my face in my hands, allowing myself to be moved and carried by the work's impressions on me.

The reasons why my responses to this gallery were so powerful include the striking sense of intentionality and presence in every shape and scribble of Twombly's work. The design of the gallery itself was, in part, the work of Twombly, along with that of the architect Renzo Piano. The building is modern and understated. Certain gallery rooms incorporate wood benches, inviting stillness or contemplation. Others seem almost to challenge the visitor to keep from hurrying through, enticed by a view of a dramatic piece displayed in the next room.

Is this gallery—its structure, composition, and artwork—a transmission of Cy Twombly himself? Was I stepping through the rooms of his consciousness? Was I sensing his devotion? His inspiration? His love?

Sara would say that I was experiencing precisely those things. "To the extent that mindful and loving hands are engaged in the design and construction process of a building," she would explain, "those who later live or work in that building will, consciously or unconsciously, sense that love and mindfulness as a part of their experience of the building." The collective resonance of the building and all that it contains moved me, activated an aliveness in my soul, and left me in a state of profound gratitude.

It is the feminine-receptive aspect of our consciousness that senses the energetic and emotional transmissions (or lack of them) in the places where we live and work. Considering how removed we have become from the construction of our dwellings and the production of so many of the things we live with on a daily basis, perhaps it's not so surprising that even the most affluent among us feel a sense of disconnection and emptiness in the midst of all that we possess.

Following Tears to Tenderness

My cousin's cancer had been in remission for almost two years, but she had recently discovered a new, rapidly growing tumor in her chest. She'd returned to Houston to begin a new round of treatment, and we were alone in her hospital room for the first time since.

"I might die. Am I going to die?" She blurted it out, eyes wide.

In that moment, I felt the space of my heart throw itself open and take her in, along with the magnitude of what she felt. Tears welled in the corners of my eyes, and I could see in hers that she felt the love and openness of my presence.

She went on in a hoarse whisper, "I am not ready. There are so many things I still want to do and see. I want to see my child graduate and get married. I want to be here for my husband."

"I know you do, sweet one." I whispered back, "I know."

We then dropped into the most intimate extended silence, in which I held her hand and gently stroked her hair. We held her heartbreak together for a little while.

Jenny was younger than I was and had recently turned 50, but in that moment, I could only see her as the rail-thin, olive-skinned, curly headed girl I used to babysit each summer, along with her two siblings.

I was 11 and she was 9. As the two eldest, she and I collaborated enthusiastically on running the show as mini grown-ups. We fried eggs for breakfast, started an Elvis tribute band, constructed an extensive network of blanket and sheet tunnels, styled her three-year-old sister throughout the day, and watched every episode of *The Beverly Hillbillies.*

And every day, 30 minutes before it was time for her parents to return home, we rushed around, putting things away, washing dishes, and making beds.

I carry such fond memories of the time we had together, just after her family immigrated to the United States from London.

Eventually, our families moved to different states, but we remained close through high school and college, always excited to see each other during holidays and summer visits. After college, our paths diverged, taking us on different journeys through new relationships and far-flung towns.

At the time of this cancer recurrence, Jenny was living in Greensboro, North Carolina, with Fr. Thomas, perhaps the gentlest husband in the world, and their whip-smart teenage daughter, Marina. Thomas was serving as priest for the Dormition of the Theotokos Greek Orthodox Church, so Jenny was serving as a Presvytera (priest's wife). Our lives couldn't be more different.

I was living alone in Houston, grieving the still-fresh breakup of my longest relationship and working as a corporate management consultant.

Just a few years previously, Kimberley and I had visited Jenny and Fr. Thomas in Greensboro, staying up late in deep conversation, exchanging stories, insights, and lessons learned during our time as couples and parents.

While we had very different perspectives, our spiritual contexts were surprisingly similar. And though Jenny and I hadn't lived in the same city or spoken regularly for years, there is a way in which it always felt we had never been apart.

Jenny and I continued to share this kind of open, intimate emotional space in our time together through a very hard and fast disease progression and, eventually, through her passing. She shared her favorite memories of her daughter and husband, as well as her hopes and prayers for recovery.

Over time, as the tumors continued to grow, we wept together about the changes in her body and the difficulty in managing the physical pain. She shared her fears of death and her sadness about what she would miss. And she shared the guilt she felt about the prospect of leaving her loved ones.

We also laughed, hard. We laughed about shared memories of childhood holidays, homemade kites that wouldn't fly, and the *Beverly Hillbillies* airplane episode. We laughed about the wayward escapades of her arm, which had become unpredictable due to the pressure of the tumors.

When she was too weak or medicated to read them herself, I read to her from her religious books, breaking into a silly voice whenever I felt the ideas or stories were too simplistic or too hardline.

She giggled or smiled at me, knowing I had tremendous respect for her devotion. Nothing was off limits in our conversations. And there was always that exquisite soft silence that would descend and settle in the space around us, like a mother's embrace.

Over the course of our visits, she told me more than once that she was glad she didn't have to be careful with what she said to me. I knew what she meant, and I wish I could say that this was always a natural way of being for me, but it wasn't.

In the past, I would have had a lot to say about what she should be doing, feeling, and saying. With all the best intentions, I would have encouraged her to "stay positive," to "be strong for her family," and "to be grateful that she was in the best possible place for treatment."

None of this is bad advice, but in times of grief and sadness, we also need space to express the fullness of our feelings and emotional responses; we need to have them heard and held and to follow them wherever they lead.

Tears streamed down my face as I held Jenny's hands and stroked her face during her final hours and moments in this life.

Grief, when fully allowed and experienced, brings so much more than darkness and despair; it also brings a purity, a single-threaded kind of beauty, and a connection to the tenderness and vulnerability of our humanity. This kind of receptivity and space holding is a fundamental expression of the feminine-receptive aspect, and it recalibrates and increases our collective capacity for empathy, love, and intimacy.

It had taken me many years to develop my capacity for this kind of expression. Seven years earlier, when my son had his car accident, I had focused completely on doing, solving, thinking, and fixing. I never stopped to hold space for grief, or fear, or raw tenderness.

In the years since, I had learned through my life experiences and practices with the feminine-receptive to be still, to be quiet, to listen deeply, and to surrender and allow time and space for difficult emotions to be fully expressed and shared without interruption. I had cultivated the space for the kind of tenderness and intimacy that only grief and loss can teach.

Holding Space

The first time I heard the phrase "holding space" was after returning from the solo time of that first Vision Fast with Kimberley, just before the storytelling sessions.

Storytelling is one of the most significant aspects of the ceremony, often bringing up big emotions from past traumas, losses, or wounds.

As preparation for listening to the stories that would be shared in the circle, we were given teachings on how to "hold space" for emotional expression. The first part of the teaching involved listening "from the heart." This meant we were to receive the person's story with as much compassion as we could muster and without analyzing or formulating responses. We were to take in the whole person, beyond the words they spoke.

Intellectually, I found the instruction confusing, but when I actually tried it, I found I had no trouble at all doing it. It felt a bit like zooming out a mental camera so that instead of being completely focused on the literal meaning of the words, my mind was soft focused, taking in the words in addition to the complete essence and experience of the person before me.

In the US, we are not very practiced in the art of listening, and holding space is the purest, most authentic kind of listening. You may have heard the Scott Ginsberg quote, "Listening is not waiting to talk."

Before I received these teachings, I was one of the worst offenders in this regard. In conversations, while another spoke, I was always half listening and half formulating a pithy response in my mind.

For a time, this was useful in certain contexts and with certain people. It gave me practice integrating various points of view and presenting ideas on the fly, it sharpened my intellect, and it helped me build my credibility as a contributor in the workplace. But it was the only approach I knew, and I found it to be substantially less useful in emotionally charged interactions.

Perhaps, the most challenging of the instructions on holding space was that we were to refrain from "comforting" the person through any of the emotional responses that might emerge during the storytelling process. The guides explained that, in certain cases, the way in which we offer comfort to others can be experienced as a request for them to stop feeling what they feel. And the truth is, for some of the more sensitive among us, either consciously or unconsciously, that is exactly the request. In addition to our very real compassion for their pain and our wish for them to be comforted, we also want them to feel better because their suffering is difficult for us to witness.

We tell them "it will be okay." We explain the reasons why it's not so bad. We remind them how much there is to be grateful for. And when they feel better, we all feel better.

On the receiving end, I have found it tremendously helpful and comforting to have another person hold space for me. As a sensitive child who'd ingrained the pattern of dissociating from my emotions in order to blend in, I am strongly attuned to the cues of others. If I sense my emotional expression is making someone uncomfortable, I can snap back into my head losing access to my feelings. So in learning to hold space for others, I have also learned to hold space for my own emotions and to become more accepting and comfortable with my own feelings.

In the practice of holding space, instead of comforting, we provide a safe zone where emotions can be expressed and followed through to their resolution. This does not apply to abusive or aggressive emotional expressions, which are in no way tolerated. We allow whatever feelings to come without interruption. We compassionately allow the speaker's sadness or pain to be whatever it is, unjudged, unanalyzed, and unevaluated.

As I have worked with the practice of holding space, or deep listening, my conversations have become richer and more authentic, and my relationships have deepened in intimacy.

This sort of listening expands the territory of the relationship and increases the level of trust, respect, and understanding such that any one misstep or argument no longer represents a threat. Disagreements or miscommunications feel less personal and less serious, more like minor blips at the surface of much deeper waters.

Occasionally, I am asked what steps I would recommend to those wishing to learn this way of relating. Holding space can only really be learned by practicing deep listening and authentic communication with a group. I suggest searching for groups that practice "Authentic Relating Games," "The Way of Council," or "Circling." Some psychotherapists also lead Process Groups, which also provide opportunities to learn and practice holding space.

There is no fixed program for learning to be in deep communion or hold space for others. Generally, I believe that we should tune in to what calls us, following our own sparks of curiosity, intuition, and interest to find groups and experiences that feel right for us. After all, if we all learn to listen for what calls us, we're already becoming more receptive. And if we're learning to be more receptive, we're already learning to hold space.

Spiraling into Beauty

Slightly off center in the black and white video, Sara's face was peaceful and luminous. The designer who'd taught me so much about the creation of mindful, nurturing spaces was discussing beauty.

An off-screen voice prompted her, "Tell me about beauty.... How do you experience beauty?"

A slight smile crossed her lips as she began. "Beauty can be in a thing...but it is not the thing. It's the noticing...and the awareness...and the gratitude...and the devotion...and the love...the nature made manifest. It's a communion...you feel it...you don't see it...you can't make it, really...but you can let it be and you can observe it...you can't possess it...it's always moving...it's spirit...and those energies or intentions can create something...and you can feel it from the thing that was created...but it's not the material itself...it's the meeting of what's physical and nonphysical...you can feel it...and be aware of it... but you can't chase it and possess it and find fulfillment in it... you can devote yourself to it...."

Sara's voice carried both a palpable delight and a relaxed meditative quality throughout the 30 minutes of this spoken exploration of the experience of beauty. Watching it, this video took me on a journey that was in turn meditative, hypnotic, and illuminating.

For the first 10 minutes or so, I felt my logical mind grappling to understand it in a linear way, to take it in and analyze the words, as if it were a conversation, as if a case were being made. But the only structure that I could manage to infer from the flow of words was the spiral thrum that the question again and again revisited, "How do you experience beauty?"

My mind eventually shifted into a relaxed and receptive state, allowing itself to be immersed in the flow of the words and informed by their impressions.

I was left with the feeling that I had received a kind of download of awareness directly into my consciousness in a way that completely bypassed my analytical brain and gave me a much greater and more complete understanding of the felt sense of beauty.

Ever since this experience, I have become engaged in a rich kind of sensory conversation with the world on the mystery of beauty, opening me to transcendent moments that, previously, would not have been available to me.

Merriam-Webster defines beauty as, "the quality or aggregate of qualities in a person or thing that gives pleasure to the senses or pleasurably exalts the mind or spirit."

As definitions go, it's not bad. I mean, it's a handy reference for a term paper, but it's not a definition that approaches the richness of the felt experience of beauty. It's brief and linear. And it's incomplete. It gives us no hints as to where beauty comes from or the conditions under which this "exalting of mind or spirit" is experienced. It leaves unsaid the ways in which beauty can be so vast and yet also so particular, how it can be so universal and yet so individual.

In her book, *Addiction to Perfection*, Jungian analyst Marion Woodman writes, "Linear thinking does not come naturally to me; moreover, it kills my imagination. Nothing happens. No bell rings. No moment of HERE and NOW. No moment that says YES. Without those moments, I am not alive. And, so, rather than driving toward a goal, I prefer the pleasure of the journey through a spiral."[9]

I had come to experience and appreciate this pleasure myself, through the spiraling word explorations of my most receptive and freewheeling friends. Walking in Silver Spring, Maryland, on a January morning, my friend, Jen, pulled her quilted jacket tighter around her neck and exhaled a shiver. Her face was alive and red from the cold, smiling into the camera she was holding.

She had posted a new video and—even though I was thousands of miles away—I felt myself walking with her.

9   Woodman, Marion. *Addiction to Perfection* (Inner City Books; 1st Ed. Canada Edition January 31, 1982).

She began, "What if devotion isn't a decision? ...what if it's a way of life? ...a way of being? ...and a way of loving someone? ...what if it's a mindset? ...or a way of seeing? ...what if it's not a way of doing...but a way of being? ...what if it's a form of attention? ...what if it's an expression of your focus? ...what if it's not about your behavior? ...what if it's about your becoming? I believe we can listen to what's rising from our deep within...it's a different kind of practice...less trying...more noticing...more raw being with...less judging the sharp edges...more power...gentle, strong, honest power...from tender true places...."

And so I traveled with Jen through a spiraling exploration of the question, "What is devotion?" Jen was not really looking to "define" devotion. She was not writing a doctoral thesis or making a case or preparing a pitch for an episode of *Shark Tank*. She was not searching for "the answer" to the question. She was riffing, improvising on a theme to see where the experience might take her and any companions who might have chosen to come along for the ride.

This way of articulating a question and allowing an intuitive insight to emerge as an inspired assertion before returning again and again and again to the same question provides us a wonderfully clear example of the beauty in a balance of the feminine-receptive and the masculine-assertive. Practices like this can grow and enrich our understanding and awareness and enable us to live more fully into our life experiences. I think of this kind of verbal exploration as a spiral, rather than a circle, because every time we return to the question we are asking it from a more informed or deeper place that has been made possible by how it's been given voice. The feminine expression receives the inspiration, and the masculine expression—in the form of a verbal assertion through the voice—moves us to a new place where we may ask again.

There is no real way to define devotion or beauty with the brevity of the conventional definitions most appreciated in a western cultural context. Until I listened to Sara speak about beauty or Jen riff on devotion, I had never taken the time to recognize how limited the dictionary definitions of these words are.

These women have given themselves permission to express themselves verbally in ways that are out of alignment with the linear and logical expectations and preferences of our western culture.

As someone who studied for a degree in literature and loves poetry, I appreciated how these friends brought verbal improvisation as a practice into their daily lives without feeling the need to apologize for it.

In so many conversations, there is much meaning left on the table. There is no need to explore every topic this way, but so many of our conversations are perfunctory. We tend to ask and answer from an almost predictable repertoire of questions that focus on life's activities and goals, such as, "How's work?" or "What is Kris doing after graduation?" or "What are you doing this weekend?"

I have come to treasure teachings that arrive in spirals like this. They add dimension to my understanding and heighten my sensitivity to the nuances of feeling that certain words reach and strain to express.

But I admit that not so very long ago, I would have wanted to interrupt this dreamy, wordy exploration. I would likely have felt frustrated waiting for the answer. Only love and politeness would have kept me from blurting out something like, "Jen! Where is this going? What exactly are you trying to say about devotion? What do you want us *to do?*"

Now I get it. I don't interrupt.

As I consider what it is about these verbal explorations that makes them so rich and impactful, I sense part of it is that they are not bound to conform to the usual expectations of rationality and linearity. There is a relaxed curiosity about them, a comfort with not knowing the answer, and a lack of attachment to accuracy or logical coherence. The exploration is not exactly stream-of-consciousness because, while the ideas emerge spontaneously, they remain anchored to the initiating question. This anchoring, this consistent return to the same question, is what imbues these verbal adventures with the sense of spiraling.

Each time we are brought back to the question before being taken around again, the sensation is that we are approaching the question from a new place, a place of enhanced awareness, rather than the place we started. We are *integrating and growing or deepening our understanding as we go.*

As we learn to value, embrace, and experiment with simple spiral explorations like this, alone and in the company of others, we will begin to recognize how this kind of balance feels in the mind, body, and spirit. And that balance of opening to receive inspiration and then knowing the beauty of bringing that inspiration into the world through the actions of our bodies…well isn't that what we're here for?

Turning and Turning

Because we are in the habit of valuing the more logical and linear expression associated with the masculine-assertive, we can easily become impatient with the sometimes slower and less certain spiral trajectory of the more balanced expression.

And if we use this spiraling approach to communicate a grocery list (and I have a few friends who have that tendency), it can be more than a little frustrating to those on the receiving end.

But this balance of the feminine-receptive and the masculine-assertive aspects provides us the inspiring capacity for a depth and breadth of exploration and integration of the mysteries of mind, body, and spirit. And that capacity brings with it the potential to inform and enrich our earthly walks with a fullness that cannot be approached through logic and linearity alone.

So give yourself more time and space for receiving. Follow the invitations that most call to you. Look for opportunities to engage and cultivate friendships with artists and activists and poets and agitators, people who make nontraditional choices in how they communicate and live and work. Follow them online, in studios, on nontraditional farms, and on alternative podcasts.

Allow an impossible question to flash into your own awareness and let yourself follow it through your own spiral of answers. Invite children and other willing explorers to join you.

While I am personally more likely to use a logical and linear approach in my verbal communication, the same kind of spiral has always been a regular part of my process for consuming, integrating, and synthesizing information into a more multidimensional understanding.

This process usually begins with an intense spark of intuition and curiosity related to a concept or a controversy or a public person, or sometimes, even all of these.

Essentially, I follow this inspiration wherever it takes me, and it often takes me well off the beaten path; I'm likely to spend hours identifying and digging into minor associations and lateral connections and peripheral concepts in a variety of ways, always eventually circling back to the original impulse for my curiosity. For me, this spontaneous, spiral journey can continue for days or weeks or months, and the topics have ranged from blockchain architecture and Vitalik Buterin to Carl Jung and dream analysis to trauma responses and the neuroscience of dance to Jim Carrey, New Orleans Bounce, and cryptography.

Besides making my life more fascinating to me and expanding the depth and range of my understanding of certain concepts, this spiraling exploration seems to allow my mind to discover and process consistencies, overlaps, and similarities in seemingly completely unrelated areas. This approach has been a great benefit to me in my work life, equipping me to anticipate broad trends and to position myself and my clients to be better prepared for them. Processing and integrating diverse information and experiences in this way equips me with rare insights that would not be available to me if I stayed on the linear logical path to understanding.

Lying on Couches

My friend, Jen, of the devotion spiral, is a gifted, heart-centered, writer-artist, intuitive, and nurturer, who works as a mentor and guide to people who are grieving loss or passing through difficult transitions.

Once, as I was introducing her to other friends, I asked her to tell them a little about her work. She said, "Well I lie on the couch a lot.... I listen to people's stories and take long walks...and sometimes I write...."

I swiveled my head around and gave her an incredulous look. This description was, in my opinion, an obscene diminishment of the nature of her work. Trying to compensate, I quickly sputtered out some additional descriptions that included words like "magic," "soulful," and "rites of passage."

Her unassuming description of her work shouldn't have surprised me. Jen doesn't regard her work as purely a business. She makes her writing available at no cost and often provides free mentoring and coaching to clients who cannot afford to compensate her. Because of that generosity, she consistently struggles to generate enough income to pay her bills.

When I first met her, I found myself at times frustrated with what I perceived as her unwillingness to clearly articulate the nature of her work, to market her services, to compile her writings into a book, and to leverage her substantial gifts for her own financial gain..

But over time, I have come to a deeper understanding of the nature of her work and her motivations. And I also began to understand my frustration as another way in which I had internalized our cultural systemic bias toward the masculine-assertive expression.

Our economic system values directed action and rewards productivity. Successful writers and artists are defined and valued by how prolific they are and by the market value of the work they've sold.

Much of Jen's work resides in the feminine-receptive expression. She receives people spiritually and emotionally, she listens and holds space for the grieving and the disenfranchised, she writes heart- and spirit-centered stories of connection and shares them freely over her social media channels, and she encourages her readers to imagine a future in which we appreciate our togetherness more than our separation.

In a very real way, she doesn't see her life and destiny as distinct from that of her clients. For that matter, she doesn't see her life and destiny as distinct or separate from that of the global community.

Jen actively resists any model that would value individuality over community or separateness over togetherness. In other words, she declines to sign on for our prevailing cultural values and economic systems, which exclusively affirm and reward the masculine-assertive aspects of individuality and exceptionalism.

Friends like Jen remind me that the value of what is most worthwhile in this life is not measured by most of the ways in which our culture defines success, and this perspective has been immensely helpful to me as I look to live a more balanced, meaningful, and inspired life.

Our existing cultural models provide a practical framework for individual material success, but they don't consider or serve the nurturing of our interdependence with other beings or with the planet as a whole.

When we maintain such a narrow vision that we see our individual success and comfort as complete and separate from everyone and everything else, we ignore fully half of who and what we are, and we do so at our own peril. We are not sustainable as individual beings in the absence of our ecosystems and communities. And we have barely scratched the surface of understanding the degree to which we are all connected on a psychic, emotional, and spiritual level. When we can hold in our awareness that our existence is equally individual (masculine-assertive) and interdependent (feminine-receptive), we will naturally create more compassionate and life-affirming systems that serve a more just and beautiful future.

Out of Balance: Logic and Reason

As a society, we are suffering from a lack of ability to empathize with the experience of those who hold different beliefs and opinions.

Ten minutes spent watching the current congressional debates or a quick look at the landscape of social media goes a long way toward showing us what's missing. Whether the topics are an upcoming election, racial equality, or the minimum wage, Americans seem increasingly challenged to receive and empathize with those whose experiences and perspectives are different from our own.

We are completely unpracticed at listening deeply or holding emotional space for others. Our ever-more polarized interactions focus more on having the "winning" argument than on listening deeply in order to connect, relate, and become more fully informed about the experience of another.

Unwittingly, we use logic and reason as the means for denying the emotional truths and lived experiences of those in pain. Presented with a different perspective, we are quick to re-center our own experience and defend it as true, often by focusing exclusively on the information that lends credence to our point of view. For example, when a Black man relates his lived experience of racial biases in policing, many are quick to counter their own experiences, along with select statistics and stories to demonstrate that this experience is not representative of "all police."

For the purposes of the argument, the Black man's pain and his in-the-bones, emotional knowing that many of his engagements with law enforcement over the course of his life have been tainted by racial bias are dismissed as irrelevant and unprovable.

In order for us to have the real, connected conversations necessary to solve our most pressing and emotionally charged problems, we must begin to receive more fully and empathize with those whose perspectives, feelings, and experiences are vastly different from our own.

The feminine-receptive aspect allows that there are other valid kinds of truth besides a predominance of facts and there are likewise other valid ways of knowing what is true and right besides following a trail of logical breadcrumbs to their rational end point. Some truth we simply know because we feel it in our hearts. When others hurt, we hurt. When the needs of others are met, we feel more ease.

In a recent conversation about politics with my son, he asked me, "How do you even have a conversation about politics right now? If you make a case that the president is corrupt and amoral, presenting evidence of specific documented incidents and lies he's told, his supporters will argue that this is true of all politicians and present a different set of facts to back up their point of view."

I owned up to not knowing the answer. What I do know is that there is tremendous power in expressing the pure truth of our feelings. When we can learn to speak from the heart about what hurts, frustrates, inspires, and moves us, we can begin to generate openings to a deeper kind of communion with others.

Speaking from our emotional truth is a vulnerable thing to do. We risk that others may bully us for our perceived weakness, but no one can argue the truth of what we feel in our hearts or sense in our nervous systems.

We do a lot of intellectual word parsing and use logical one-up-manship to advance our point of view. If we're good at arguing, we can use that talent to win every argument, but winning arguments does not improve conditions or inspire happiness. To accomplish those things, we have to get better at listening to, receiving, and connecting with others to cocreate workable solutions.

We repeat the values we've been taught—that no good can come from attending to unpleasant experiences or emotions, that it's best for those in pain to put bad feelings aside and pull themselves together, and that they are lucky it isn't worse. On a societal scale, we see logic and reason used as the basis of arguments that would have us believe that there are simple, impassive solutions to our most emotionally layered, complex, and nuanced problems. None of our most significant and challenging problems—problems such as race relations, environmental degradation, poverty, and health care—will be solved by any program or argument that does not involve deep, empathic listening and emotional space holding.

What might be possible in our communities, workplaces, and country if we improved our capacity for this kind of listening? How might this practice improve our ability to approach conversations on charged issues?

What would happen if, instead of attempting to redirect or fix, we learned to compassionately hold space for those in pain? Let's imagine and allow ourselves to feel hopeful about the breakthroughs that could be possible if we were to find ways to incorporate deep, receptive listening as primary to our approach of problem-solving.

Practices:
Heart-Centered Listening and Empathic Space Holding

In conversations, we often have so many ideas and words to express that we attend only superficially to the words of others. If we practice the art of receiving, of listening first with our full and devoted attention, we may be surprised by our capacity to take in the feelings, thoughts, and ideas of others.

This can be a very challenging practice for those of us raised and educated in western culture, with its focus on expediency and efficiency of expression. But learning to receive others in this way will open us to greater compassion and intimacy in our relationships, even with those whose perspectives are vastly different.

Practice receptivity. Commit a day to silence. Only listen, and listen deeply. Avoid distracting yourself with electronics and other entertainment. Practice giving your utmost attention to everything in your midst, without commenting on it. Read the news, listen to lunch conversations, and sit through meetings, allowing your reactions to come and go.

If you must communicate something important, write it down. Notice anything you may have been missing, and take a few minutes to journal your reactions at the end of the day.

For many, perhaps even for most of us, it can be unsettling to remain emotionally present in the midst of those experiencing intense sadness. We want to help, to cheer them up, to relieve them of their pain. We want to give them advice, to remind them of the good things, to snap them out of it.

It is not easy to bear witness to those we care about in their times of grief, but beautiful moments of compassion and connection emerge for those who learn to do so.

Visit a relative or friend who is grieving a significant loss. Practice "holding space" for the person, allowing them to express the fullness of their sadness and to tell their stories without interruption or judgment. Resist any urge to change the subject, give advice, or cheer them up. Require nothing. Allow silence. Make tea. Show interest in any stories they choose to tell. Sit quietly and take them in.

Our culture reinforces in us the habit of listening with the intent to respond, an intent to win at conversation, to say the right thing and to say it first and with confidence. This habit keeps us from experiencing the expressions and perspectives of others fully; it keeps us removed from a state of true receptivity.

Learning the practice of deep listening can transform relationships, creating deeper understanding, intimacy, and unprecedented opportunities for co-creation and collaborative problem-solving.

Practice deep listening. Invite an acquaintance who has lived a very different experience from you to coffee or dinner. Explain that your intention is just to ask questions and to more fully understand his or her perspective. Prepare a few questions ahead of time in case you need them, but also allow yourself to be intensely curious and see what follow-up questions emerge naturally.

Allow the conversation to progress organically as much as possible. Ask for stories to deepen your understanding. Occasionally mirror back what you have heard to ensure your understanding is accurate. Specifically listen for emotional connections, and notice any reactions you experience in response. Allow silence for reflection and processing as needed. Resist any urge or prompting to share your own perspective or realizations; propose a different meeting for that if desired.

Make sure to thank the person for the opportunity to know them better. The true challenge is this: repeat this entire process with others for the rest of your life.

CHAPTER 7

Sending Up a Flare

Camping with Millennials

The loud whisper came from behind me, "Hey, are you leaving us?"

I turned around to see Tami, a young professional woman in her twenties, standing in my cubicle.

"Well, what do you mean?" I replied, smiling.

Looking around in mock-conspiracy, she went on. "Take me with you! I'm dying in here!"

Laughing, my voice and heart full of affection, I told her, "Okay, yes. I will find a job for you…as soon as I find one for me."

By this point, I'd been working on a consulting gig within this large energy company for a couple of years. During my time there, I had the opportunity to collaborate with and coach a few young people. Tami was one of them.

She was an honors graduate out of a top-tier university and was actively recruited into this well-respected Fortune 500 Company. She made a very good salary, was provided an excellent benefits package, and was part of a high-profile rotational training program on a fast track to a leadership role. And she was completely uninspired by her work.

It's not that she didn't understand the opportunity she was being provided or that she took the income and benefits for granted. It was simply that she was not inspired by the mission of the corporation, which—for this and for all companies listed on our public exchanges—is to grow profitability.

During my time there, Tami and I developed a trusting relationship, one in which we openly discussed current events, social, global, and environmental issues, as well as our concerns and wishes for the future. She shared her tremendous frustration with the ways in which young people of her generation, the millennials, are frequently disparaged by those in the generations that entered the workplace before them.

And I got it. As the parent of a 25-year-old son, I had developed a great appreciation and compassion for the challenges faced by millennials in the workforce. During one of our lunch conversations, I admitted to Tami that, while I believe my generation has done a lot of things right, we hadn't done enough, in my opinion, to fix our flawed economic systems.

"The way I see it," I told her, "my generation did a lot to instill in you, our children, the millennials, some solid altruistic values. We wanted you to learn to solve problems collaboratively, to look out for your neighbors, to recycle, and to take care of the environment and the natural world, to look for meaningful and inspiring ways to use your talents, and to try to make the world a better place—and you learned those things well. However," I continued, "we didn't do enough to reform our economic systems to reward those altruistic values in practice."

In the US, our economic systems reward growth of profit over any other value. This dynamic is clearly reflected in quarterly earnings calls, annual reports, and price charts of the companies traded on our public stock exchanges. Our institutions and investors demonstrate a consistent preference for purchasing and retaining the stock of corporations that consistently grow profits, regardless of the destructive impacts their business operations have on communities, public health, and the environment.

And through the miracle of the Internet, our young people have grown up seeing the effects of those profit-driven systems on communities and ecosystems, not just in the US but around the world.

My generation came of age and entered the workforce without much awareness of the impact of our growth-driven systems. I had no easy way of finding out who manufactured my stereo. I made it through most of my twenties without having any reason to question the relative greatness of my country's economic models and systems.

By contrast, the kids of today have a front row seat to observe the ever-increasing impacts. They see and feel the impacts of our consumerist culture and profit-first models on the planet. Many have seen their parents laid off, after decades of loyal service to a corporation, following a bad quarterly report or an economic downturn. Others are buried in college loan debt that may take decades to pay off. And most are keenly aware that wages have become stagnant, requiring them to work more hours than their parents to maintain a lower standard of living.

They have seen the impact of these systems on the natural environment. They know who builds their smartphones and the conditions in which those people live and work. I don't find it the slightest bit surprising that some of the more sensitive among them want to opt out, escaping into Netflix and camping out in their parents' basements.

Targets and Trade-Offs

At the end of our working careers, will it be enough for us to say that we spent most of our lives working for a corporation that consistently grew profit but, in the process, made the planet less livable for the coming generations? This is what's happening, and we all feel the truth of this on some level, consciously or unconsciously, because we are undeniably interdependent with this planet and everything that lives on it.

The mission of growing profit every year is not noble enough, not just for millennials but for any of us. And I feel confident saying this, not only because it's so abundantly obvious but because I have observed the disillusionment among so many of my peers, even those who have generated significant success in these systems. I recall a poignant conversation with the executive leader of a multibillion-dollar business unit within a multinational energy company. Brent was one of the most inspirational leaders I had encountered in my career as a consultant. He had invested significant time and budget in offsite meetings with his team to develop a set of shared values and performance goals. One of the values his team had agreed to was protecting the environment. As a related performance goal, they had collectively decided they would not "flare" while they were producing hydrocarbons. Flaring is a common practice of burning off natural gas while producing oil from a well; the practice releases pollutants into the atmosphere.

Just a few months later, when I arrived at Brent's office for our check-in, I saw him sitting with his head in his hands. When I asked him if everything was okay, he told me that his team was unhappy with him because he was forced to override their collective goal. He had issued them a directive to institute flaring in some of their operations. The team had experienced unexpected delays due to technical problems and were off-track with their production schedule. Now they had to fast-track their operations to get back on schedule, and this meant that they would not be able to avoid flaring. He looked at me, clearly dismayed by the choice he felt he had to make.

He said, "I am completely aligned with my team in wanting to limit our environmental impact, but our business unit is responsible for 20 percent of the company's financial projections for this year. Frankly, if we don't hit our numbers, I won't have a job next year. I don't have a choice about this, but they don't understand. They think I haven't gone to bat for them."

After this turn of events, I never again saw in Brent or his team the enthusiasm, pride, and cohesiveness that had previously been so inspiring to witness. And this conversation is just one of many examples of situations in which I have seen executive leaders of some of the world's largest corporations compelled to make decisions that were neither in line with their personal values nor in service to the good of the environment or community—all so they would meet their company's ever-increasing, profit-growth targets.

Out of Balance: One-Sided Stories

Cultures are built and carried forward by their stories. Our cultural values frame and color the ways in which we see and tell our hero stories. In the US, these stories consistently emphasize the ideals of individuality and individual power, fierce competition, intellect, directed action, and emotional impassivity—all aspects of the masculine-assertive expression.

At the same time, either directly or by omission, the stories of our heroes minimize the significance of important relationships and collaborations, intuition and receptivity, influence of the arts, and physical and emotional sensitivity.

We especially favor the story of the scrappy immigrant who arrived in this country with nothing but the clothes on his back and who bootstrapped himself into prominence and wealth with no help from those around him. He is hard-nosed, independent, action-oriented, and smart. He married a practical woman, started a business young, worked 70 hours a week, smoked like a chimney, spanked his kids when they needed it, didn't have time to wallow in his feelings, and didn't tolerate those who did. Of course, all historical, family, and business stories are more complex and nuanced than the versions we typically hear, but that is the point.

We value winners and winning. Our news stories focus on who's winning in everything from sports to business to entertainment to politics. Reality television makes new winners for us to celebrate every season. Our business news heralds stock market winners, with magazines and websites making celebrities out of their CEOs.

We even publish lists of those who have accumulated the most wealth. We treat nearly everything as a contest, celebrating those who come out on top regardless of the collateral damage. At the country level, we even track and review our Gross Domestic Product rates to see which countries are winning the contest of producing the most stuff.

We could look at this trend as a natural extension of our cultural bias to perceive ourselves (our families, our companies, our country) as separate from others, without the balance of recognizing the degree to which we are all connected and interdependent. This perspective feeds an overemphasis on competition and hoarding, rather than on collaboration and sharing.

In balance, healthy competition is a good thing. It can keep us focused on improving and make us physically stronger and mentally sharper. When out of balance, however, competition becomes toxic. To understand the impact of toxic competition, we need look no further than our political processes.

Each election season, billions of dollars are poured into political campaigns, which are increasingly treated less as opportunities for us all to learn about and select our public servants and more as no-holds-barred personal battles by candidates to "win" a position in political office. Insults are hurled. Bridges are burned. Polarization becomes baked into our most important conversations.

Our social media applications and newsfeeds bombard us with headlines, whether it is the latest scathing criticism of the president of the United States, a charged statement about the socialist dangers of universal health care, or provocative pictures of those protesting racial injustice, many of us get sucked into the battlefield and engage in similar behavior with friends and neighbors. This kind of competition makes us neither stronger nor sharper. And even when we're certain we came out on top in the argument, winning doesn't make us happier.

According to the longest study on happiness, conducted by Harvard University over the course of almost 80 years, positive relationships and embracing community are the keys to both happiness and longevity.[10]

Natalie Boyd quotes a more recent study: "There are three main things that make people happy: Close relationships, a job or pastime that they love, and helping others. On the other hand,

10 Liz Mineo, "Over Nearly 80 Years, Harvard Study Has Been Showing How to Live a Healthy and Happy Life," Harvard Gazette, November 26, 2018, https://news.harvard.edu/gazette/story/2017/04/over-nearly-80-years-harvard-study-has-been-showing-how-to-live-a-healthy-and-happy-life/.

money and material things do not have a lot to do with happiness, and those who emphasize them are not."[11]

Given that American culture is so closely identified with both individualism and capitalism, it's no surprise that the US does not rank as high in the World Happiness Report as one might expect, despite our relative wealth and influence.

Finland consistently ranks at the top of the list, followed by Denmark, Switzerland, Iceland, and Norway. The report highlights as key findings: "That people like living in communities and societies with less inequality of well-being, and where trust—of other people and of public institutions—is high. People in high-trust communities are much more resilient in the face of a whole range of challenges to their well-being: illness, discrimination, fear of danger, unemployment, and low income. Just to feel that they can count on others around them, and on their public institutions, makes their hardships less painful, thereby delivering benefits to all and especially those most in need."[12]

As humans sharing a planet with each other and with all other life, there is a level at which we also share a destiny. It's important to remember that we are wired for collaboration and cooperation every bit as much as we are for competition and individuality. Let's imagine how our stories might be different if we learn to value the process of co-creating a healthy and hopeful future as much as we value winning.

---

11 Natalie Boyd, "Research on Happiness: What Makes People Happy?," Study. com, https://study.com/academy/lesson/research-on-happiness-what-makes-people-happy.html.

12 Katia Hetter, "During a Pandemic, What Does Being the World's Happiest Country Mean?," CNN, March 20, 2020, https://www.cnn.com/travel/article/worlds-happiest-country-wellness-2020/index.html.

Practices:
The Whole Story

Even those of us who think of ourselves as easygoing and flexible can get locked into an unbalanced perspective. There are at least a few positions on which we are unyielding, a couple of contentious issues on which we are certain that our position represents the irrefutable truth. Perhaps, our position is based on an emotional sensitivity to the issue. Maybe it is shaped by a spiritual understanding. Or perhaps, instead, it's drawn from a logical analysis of the facts of the matter. When we lock into a viewpoint without allowing space for balance or curiosity about the perspectives of others, we limit our ability to more completely and compassionately apprehend the fullness of the issue. We also limit our ability to work with those who hold different perspectives to generate creative solutions to our problems.

Agree to agree. Review an argument in which you have a definitive point of view and do some research. Read articles, watch videos, and search the Internet to find a point of agreement with one or more opposing points of view. Look for value in alternative perspectives. This practice may require a significant stretch—the more we stretch, the more effective the practice. Notice your emotions and physical sensations throughout this process. Whether we agree or disagree with others on an issue, they have reasons for their positions, and it can be truly expansive to learn to see the same challenge from multiple perspectives. Make note of your emotions throughout this exercise and of any new possibilities that come to mind. While I consider myself compassionately pro-choice on the issue of abortion, my perspective on this emotionally charged issue was expanded after making the conscious effort to listen deeply to the specific objections and to hold space for the pain of those who consider themselves pro-life. It can seem as if some of our most challenging conversations have become frozen in time, as if those on either side of the issue are repeating old talking points and the dialog is not allowed to move in ways that are either constructive or creative. For me, this exercise changed the way I approach and discuss the issue of abortion, and my conversations on the topic have become more generative and sensitive. I am convinced we could be having better conversations if we learned to listen for and integrate the truth and validity in "the other" perspective.

We tend to see our heroes through the filters and biases of our cultural systems. In the US, this means we emphasize and celebrate the masculine-assertive aspects of our heroes; we focus on the actions they took, their intellect and rationality, and the narrative of their toughness and competitive triumphs over adversity and adversaries. These biases in our hero stories keep us from seeing the greater context of their lives, including the ways in which the feminine-receptive aspects may also have shaped and sustained their successes.

Look for balance in your heroes. Find heroes, past and present, who express a balance of "be" and "do," of receptivity and action, of sensitivity and rationality. Learn their stories and share them. Dig deep and consider specifically the ways in which their feminine-receptive expression influences or informs their actions. Do they demonstrate an uncommon intuition? Are they known for fostering collaboration? Has their sensitivity or capacity for compassion made them more effective leaders? What makes the actions they take in the world inspiring to you?

Research and consider their frailties and mistakes. In recognizing the fullness of their humanity, we can more fully relate to and appreciate their accomplishments with balance and compassion.

One of my personal heroes is environmental activist, author, and scholar, Joanna Macy. For me, she represents a beautiful balance of the feminine-receptive and masculine-assertive expressions. Her book, *Coming Back to Life*, has reminded me how to open to feeling and connection (the feminine-receptive) as a basis for informing inspired, life-affirming actions (the masculine-assertive). I recommend a read.

CHAPTER 8

My Life in the Balance

Morning Balancing Practice

Realizing I'd slept later than I intended, I squinted at my phone. I hadn't even stood up and I was already thinking about my list and feeling behind schedule. I closed my eyes, centered myself, and breathed deeply. I can still feel the pull to head straight to the shower and start getting things done. But I have learned not to do this most of the time. Things go better for me if I start the day with 30 minutes to an hour of allowing and receiving.

These days that typically means lighting candles in my small altar space and then moving through a combination of body warm-ups, breath-work (pranayama), the yoga practice of Bound Lotus, and intuitive movement with prayers of gratitude and invitations for guidance. I have been practicing kundalini yoga and meditation on and off for over 20 years now. And while I have always recognized and appreciated the benefits of this practice, until recently it could still feel like another thing on my to-do list.

The basic practice of bringing awareness to the breath initiates a balancing of receptive and expressive energies. So combining breathwork with intention activates a natural physical balancing that serves also to remind the psyche of balancing the feminine -receptive with the masculine-assertive.

As I have become more attuned to what moves and opens me, I no longer follow every teaching I have received to the letter. Instead, I allow myself intuitively to combine and shape the variety of practices I have studied over the years to meet what is most alive for me in the moment.

On certain days, lighting a candle and bowing my head for a few moments are enough. Certain treasured items and pictures might feel right in my meditation space on one day, and others will feel right on the next. Occasionally, I feel drawn to open and read from a random page in a book of devotionals or poetry, play Greek Orthodox monastic chanting, or offer spontaneously emerging prayers. It has become common for me to feel overcome with gratitude and love in the midst of my morning practice. This is one of the many ways my life experience has shifted as I have increasingly begun to call home my feminine-receptive expression.

The Feminine-Receptive at Work

My experiences at work have also continued to shift. In meetings with my clients and colleagues, I find myself dropping into the lessons I learned from sharing in council circles. As different people speak, I often sense something about how they are feeling along with hearing what they are saying. I interrupt less. I ask them for stories to help me understand their challenges and ideas more fully. As I listen with my full attention, I am vaguely conscious that, somehow simultaneously in the background, some part of my mind is spiraling to synthesize and integrate the various points of view.

I do more listening than ever. And when I do speak, I find I am able to share my own thoughts, feelings, and intuitions more easily and with more presence and humility. I frequently mirror back my understanding of the situation and the related issues and ask what is still missing in my interpretation.

My attachment to my ideas and designs has loosened, and I have become aware of a new openness in my perspective. This openness seems somehow to allow for others to join me in a co-creative process to play spontaneously with possibilities and generate better solutions than any one of us would have developed alone.

Of course, all of this improves my work as a consultant; it also makes my professional relationships better and more intimate. I am not consciously "doing council on my clients." It's rather that these treasured lessons I have learned from my deep communions in council circles are naturally becoming a part of how I show up with people.

Today, my clients come to trust me more quickly. They more readily share their motivations, concerns, and other details that I wouldn't otherwise know about. This deeper understanding of their needs equips me to better target my advisement and proposed solutions to support them.

Any time we deepen trust and make space for emotional vulnerability, we throw open the doors to new possibilities that will more completely address the need. This kind of authenticity, when modeled in a group or team dynamic, can create a ripple effect that amplifies trust in a broader sphere.

In a high-trust team, people are willing to take risks and stretch beyond their comfort zones to bring their best.

The Mess of Mothering

Even though I no longer have children at home, my parenting journey hasn't ended. And the feminine expression continues to teach me to become more present, more receptive, and more nurturing in my mothering. This has been one of the more stubborn aspects of myself, so I am still learning to be less occupied with doing and to create more space and opportunities for being. It's getting easier because I have experienced the beauty that can emerge when everyone learns to relax a bit in the flow and mess of life (and I have made my share of life messes).

I have grown more to understand that not everything needs to be structured and planned.

If we leave space for spontaneity, if we leave the musical instruments out, if we assist in the lemon experiment, if we allow the piercing, sometimes the most joyful magic can happen—musicals, discoveries, benefit concerts, lemonade stands, and treasured moments of co-creativity and closeness.

Of course, I wish I had learned earlier. And I still get tripped up in my mothering and find myself doing too much telling and not enough listening or holding space. But it's getting better. The old habits are loosening, and I am faster to notice and self-correct and more comfortable apologizing when I get off track. And I count myself most fortunate to be considered a mother or godmother by a few of the most gracious of humans.

A Presence of Heart

As I have engaged with the work to reclaim and balance my full expression, I have noticed changes in all my relationship dynamics. I recently ran into an old friend at a school performance for one of my godchildren.

When we greeted each other, I noticed he was working hard keep an even facial expression. I recognized this as one of his ways of coping with years of chronic physical pain and regular bouts of depression. In that moment, more so than ever before, I felt an enormous wave of compassion wash over me, which brought tears to my eyes. I sat next to him, and I continued to allow myself to sense his struggle and to hold space for him throughout the performance. We didn't speak about it, but I know he felt it.

I have known Ben for over 20 years, and I regret to say that I am only just recently connected enough to my own emotional life to experience this degree of empathy for his challenges.

The interaction stayed with me well after I returned home, and I continued to feel into it, eventually performing a kind of mental review of my relationship with him through the years.

I felt such remorse that my own dissociation had rendered me so incapable, for so long, of sharing a compassionate presence with him in his times of pain. This shift has changed the dynamic of my relationship with Ben. While I am not sure whether the shift is obvious from the outside, I notice it as an increased sense of ease in our interactions. And though we haven't talked about it, I also know that Ben senses the difference.

This kind of remorse seems to have become a regular feature of my journey, and I do my best to allow it to teach rather than punish me.

In time, other feelings followed, including a tender compassion for myself in the knowing that I simply didn't previously have the capacity to respond in any other way and an overwhelming sense of gratitude for the realization that I am evolving ever more into aliveness.

Emotional Clumsiness

Let me hasten to add, I'm expressing more than just compassion and gratitude these days. For most of my life, I have been described as the smart, sensible, and calm one among my friends and relations; the phrase "even-keeled" has been used with some regularity. However, now that I am feeling and expressing my emotions, I am...well...feeling and expressing *all* of my emotions. This means I feel my sadness and grief and anger and frustration as well as my happiness and joy and compassion and gratitude. And the thing I've noticed about my emotions is that they come when they come, and their emergence seems often to surprise me.

So, in general, this means the ride has become bumpier and less predictable for me and for any who happen to be on the journey with me. I am still learning to allow my emotions to flow through me and inform me with grace. For example, when my anger sparks up, I do my best to listen to what it is teaching me and express it without directing it *at* anyone. But even when I am successful in this, I know it flashes in my eyes and carries in my voice and so can still be startling to both me and any in my company. And when I sense frustration building in me, I am still learning to catch it early enough to excuse myself temporarily from engagement so that I can incorporate its lessons, re-center myself, and reengage in a more productive frame of mind.

Frankly, it often feels clumsy and vulnerable to be learning, in my fifth decade, how to live in my own strong emotions. That said, I feel their lessons continuing to deepen my understanding of myself and my place in the great web of life, and I know my experiences and my relationships are vastly richer for it.

Recently, as a dear friend was making me coffee, I became suddenly overcome with gratitude for her care and presence in my life. And when she turned around to pour my coffee, she was surprised to see my eyes full of tears. Fortunately, she knows my story because I could do nothing but shrug and say through a smile, "I don't know. I'm just really grateful," and then, laughing, "Sorry I'm awkward."

From the interactions I'm having in my life now, I gather I'm much more approachable than I used to be. The less I guard and protect my feelings, the more of my own human balance I express, the more comfortable others feel sharing themselves and telling me their stories—knowing I have the capacity and compassion to receive them.

True humility cannot be faked. We sense it in people who have learned to receive their own shortcomings and show themselves compassion when they fail to live up to their own aspirations for themselves. Humility wears down our edges and opens us to more intimate connections and more deep and meaningful moments with others.

Increased Capacity

My experiences navigating my own feelings are also teaching me to be more comfortable in the midst of the strong emotional expressions of others. This means I am increasing my capacity to join people in their moments of joy and happiness and also to stay with and hold space for those experiencing major pain, grief, and anger. I've discovered that anger and grief need more avenues for healthy release.

And as long as the expressions aren't abusive, aggressive, or habituated, I no longer find them frightening, worrisome, or inappropriate. In fact, I deeply value every opportunity to hold space for these emergences, knowing they are critical for our individual and collective healing. Our most difficult emotions provide us with pathways for releasing tension, for understanding our current limits, for deepening our communion with each other, and for activating change. And my development in this way has opened me to opportunities to experience and witness stunningly beautiful moments of human connection and healing.

Embraced by the Wind

Along with increasing our capacity for intimacy and beautiful connections with others, opening ourselves more completely to sensing and experiencing our emotions also expands our capacity for awe and joy.

Embracing and remembering the feminine-receptive aspect of my psyche has recalibrated and intensified my range of experience. So, yes, my griefs are deeper and my heartbreaks more painful. But I am also overwhelmed by the beauty of sunsets and kindnesses.

I have always enjoyed walking through art galleries, reading poetry, and listening to live music, but these days I am regularly astounded by the difference in my experience of these things, compared with even a few years ago. Peak experiences like the one in the Twombly Gallery have become much more common for me as my connection with my feminine expression has become more fluid and more balanced with my masculine.

The same can be said for my encounters with the natural world. After a walk last week on Houston's city trails, I sent a text message to a friend saying, "The wind today feels like an embrace."

I wasn't exaggerating. I sense my relationship with nature in a much more intimate and visceral way than ever before. If I have been sitting indoors on my computer too much, my body tells me to go outside; these days, whenever possible, I comply. And when I do venture out, I am no longer focused on how many steps I walk or for how long.

I seldom wear my headphones because, even in the city, the birds and the bayous sing their songs and something inside me longs to hear them. I retreat regularly to the natural sanctuaries nearby to be nourished by the flashing leaves and shadows and sometimes to create land art of sticks and stones and other things found fallen on the trails. Whenever possible, I escape for weekends and weeks to wild spaces to remember myself, marveling at my connection with the fall leaves of the northeast or knowing myself as the winking moon in the southwest high desert or imagining I am a single wave in the Mediterranean waters lapping the rocky beaches of Cyprus, my mother's home country.

On the flip side, I have begun to sense just as intensely the impact of my way of life on the natural world. I feel a twinge of remorse with each bag I heave into the dumpster, deeply aware that—even though I try to make sensitive choices—I still generate far too much plastic waste.

I am no longer on a quest for perfection. I try to hold my tendency to judge myself and others with grace as I continue to grow out of my old habits. But, at the same time, I hold myself accountable for my actions and their impacts. For example, I won't beat myself up about taking an intuitive drive, but I stay in touch with the fact that this action has an impact on the planet. Holding myself accountable for the truth of that impact keeps me humble and increasingly inspires me to choose an intuitive walk over an intuitive drive.

Since air travel is a passion of mine, I no longer board a flight without considering and feeling my personal contribution to air emissions. I allow myself to feel the pinch of that impact, not as guilt, but as a knowing of my connection and interdependence—as awareness of the trade-off I am making. As the plane lifts off, I also allow myself feelings of deep gratitude and love for the planet and human ingenuity. I find seemingly small inner shifts like this create openings that can attract and allow for the emergence of new creative solutions.

Each time I notice another wild space cleared for new development, I allow myself to feel the loss of sanctuary and habitat. On days when I am feeling particularly raw, I sense it as a twist in my gut that can take me into heartbreak. As I have opened myself to feeling—emotionally and physically—the effects of my actions and of the broader trends of our species on the planet, I have felt more activated to make personal changes and also to engage with wider scale movements to find ways to reduce our collective impact.

Compassionate Divesting

As a strategic consultant to large energy corporations for over 20 years, in a significant way my entire working career has been spent contributing to the unbalanced economic and financial systems that continue to drive so much environmental degradation and waste.

Specifically, I am referring to the ways in which my work has supported the infinite profit growth objective for companies traded on our public exchanges. I do not and have not run my life in any way separate or apart from those systems. In fact, even as I have come to understand the ways in which our systems are ultimately unsustainable and destructive, I still have not figured out a way in which it is possible to live in the US and not somehow be contributing to them.

At this stage, I continue to look for effective ways to apply my compassion, skills, and energies to reform and balance these systems and to divest myself from them where and whenever possible.

I began making small but meaningful changes over a decade ago. One of my first actions was to divest myself from any stocks or bonds traded on our exchanges. At the time, that decision meant selling any individual stocks and mutual funds I had been holding in my accounts, including those in my retirement accounts.

These were not large accounts by any means, but this decision was personally significant to me because first, it eliminated at least one of the ways in which my behavior was not aligned with my personal values, and second, it represented an actual reduction of my level of investment in our unbalanced economic and financial systems. Perhaps most importantly, it presented me with a problem that I would be forced to solve creatively (i.e., how to invest in more life-affirming vehicles).

Investing in the Feminine

Over time, as I have become more conscious of the feminine-receptive expression, I found my own ways to "invest" in it.

For me, this has meant contributing to artists, ceremonialists, storytellers, nurturers, intuitives, keepers of sacred sanctuary, and other practitioners of the feminine. Sometimes I make these investments by purchasing their creations and services; other times I simply make direct financial contributions to support their work in the world. I realize this usage of the word investment is unorthodox, but I have come to believe it is the correct word.

While I don't expect a traditional financial return from these kinds of investments, I see this approach as a way for me to invest consciously in a more balanced future.

And although I am using language we typically use in a pragmatic financial context, this kind of investing has become a reverent and sacred practice for me. It's a devotional, a candle-lighting of a kind. And I feel the returns as a warming and a tending of my own inner hearth.

In recent years, I have also found methods to invest my retirement savings in ways that align more closely with the feminine. After researching investment alternatives within the little-known world of the "self-directed IRA," I bought a house situated on 12 acres of wild forest. This investment property is now held within my IRA, and any rental income goes directly back into the account.

The way I see it, besides being the owner of a piece of investment property, I am the now the caretaker and protector of 12 acres of wild space and habitat. I am continuing to explore and learn creative ways to use this type of IRA to invest in enterprises that balance the feminine and masculine aspects, but that is a longer story for a different book. Meanwhile, I do my best to remain conscious about what systems and expressions and cultural norms I support with my daily actions and my investments of time and resources.

I'm often asked if this way of investing has generated sufficient financial security for my future. The short answer is, "No." The longer answer is that I no longer believe there is such a thing as *my* financial security as something separate and apart from everything else that's happening. No sense of security can come from having millions in the bank while so many others are hungry and living in unsafe conditions.

If my investments increase my net worth but also increase environmental degradation and cause harm to others, that doesn't work for me. I feel it as the pain it is. If the effort to mitigate my own individual financial risk increases global environmental, health, and community risks, I am always going to feel the tension of those impacts. And I am never going to feel "secure" in the conditions created by this approach.

Traditional investing doesn't work for me anymore. My goals are different. I now consider the individual (masculine-assertive) and interconnected (feminine-receptive) perspectives in equal balance when making investment decisions. I hold the needs of the collective whole as equal to my individual needs; I consider the bigger picture, a picture that encompasses my children's future and that of everyone in the world.

Even writing this, I realize my tremendous good fortune in having the ability to invest in anything at all. As someone who makes my living consulting to large corporations, I acknowledge my ongoing contribution to perpetuating old, unbalanced systems. My intention here is to share a different perspective that has come only through knowing the balance of myself more completely. I claim no moral superiority or high ground.

The Magic of Maybe

Recently, I had coffee with Annie, a long-time friend and highly successful and well-respected attorney. Over the past 10 years, she's made partner in her law firm, raised three kids, served on various boards, and completed her PhD.

At one point in the conversation she said, "I'm kind of in a place where I think, 'What am I doing all this for?' I thought for a while I was doing it for my kids, but now I realize they really don't care about my achievements and the things I do. In fact, they even give me a hard time about it."

Hearing her restlessness, I asked her what she thought she might want to do next.

"I have been living to work, but I want to switch that around and work to live instead. I'm at a stage in my life when I want to work on something meaningful."

Mostly joking, I replied, "Oh, yeah, that's right...you've been doing a lot of yoga."

First, we laughed, but then we talked more seriously about consciousness, the content of this book, the bias in our systems, and balance.

At one point, seemingly out of nowhere, she said, "I could be totally into investing in some kind of organization that has as its charter the intention to research, innovate, and create together... like, without starting with an objective or an area of focus."

Smiling and nodding like a bobblehead, I responded, "Yes! I have a growing circle of friends now who are all in the same boat, Annie. We all want to go to work in organizations that don't exist yet. So maybe we've got to create them."

"Maybe" has become an operative word for me. I no longer set and hold rigid goals for my future. While I have demonstrated that I do have the ability to set goals, map their course, and make them happen, I have found that this approach requires tremendous energy and that, in the end, the achievement of the goal is often much less satisfying than I had anticipated.

This approach is taught and extolled in the US as *the way* to do things; we simply think into what would be a good next goal, and then we put our heads down and get busy doing whatever's necessary to achieve it. I have learned instead to allow the feminine-receptive aspect of my being to intuit and inform my direction.

Here's how it works for me. It starts with a flash of insight. For example, I may find myself obsessed with learning about a specific topic.

Right now, that topic is venture capital. It aligns with my ongoing search for more life-affirming approaches to investing. The possibilities for inventing new, more balanced investment models feel electric to me.

I pencil it in the back of my mind as an idea that I feel drawn to explore. Then I take another intentional step in the direction of the idea. In this case, I commit some time to internet research and order a book on venture deals.

Now I am in a process, a kind of conversation with my intuition, and I've said, "Okay, I'm listening. Now what?" And here I am again, back in the spiral that begins with a question posed by the receptive feminine and followed up with action taken by the assertive masculine.

My action keeps the energy going, equips me for conversations, and tunes my receptivity to the topic. From here, this process feels a bit like fishing. In social or professional situations, I may feel inspired to float the topic of venture capital deals and see if anyone bites. If I find an open avenue or happen to encounter potential collaborators with interest, energy, or insights on the topic, I keep taking action.

I schedule the meeting, write the email, and follow the openings. I just keep taking "the next right step." I never know exactly what "goal" I am driving toward because this process never really ends. For example, if eventually I were to collaborate on the establishment of a venture capital firm, that milestone would not represent the completion of anything. I would still be using this same process to intuit and feel my way into the next best actions as a founder of that firm.

The "inspiration first" model I've been describing engages a more balanced expression of the masculine and feminine energies than the "goal first" model we are usually taught. Staying with the venture capital example, my receptive feminine expression *first* intuits and informs, and only *then* does my assertive masculine expression direct energy and take the appropriate actions.

So my feminine aspect receives and integrates all the information about what is alive with potential and synthesizes what is needed in a given context; the masculine aspect takes directed action.

The outcomes resulting from this action then become a part of the new context, and the spiral continues. To be clear, I'm not saying this way is the right way or the only way. It's just one of my current experiments.

This way of moving in the world reminds me to stay present in every moment of my life, it allows me to remain flexible and make course corrections as needed, and it leads me on grand adventures with fascinating people—dancing through streets, biking in deserts, and cry-laughing in kitchens and conference rooms.

CHAPTER 9

Endings and Beginnings, Burnings, and Turnings

Burning in the Desert

"You should come meet me at Burning Man," laughed the voice at the other end of the line, "and it'll all get figured out."

My friend, Jennifer, and I had been on the phone for over an hour, lightheartedly freaking out together. Both of us had been steadily stepping away from solid, predictable careers (along with their accompanying solid, predictable income streams) for several months. And neither of us knew exactly what work was next. We just knew that it was coming, that it would be in service to love and healing, and that we had to make space for it.

While we'd each been on our respective paths of personal and spiritual development for years, neither of us was well-practiced at walks of faith of this magnitude, especially the kind with the potential to max out our credit cards. And it wasn't just us; each of us was aware of others in our communities stepping simultaneously across the same threshold. In a way, it felt (and continues to feel) as if we were all holding hands being brave together.

Burning Man is an annual experiment in temporary co-creative community. Each year, "Black Rock City" is constructed in the dusty Black Rock Desert of Nevada, about 100 miles northeast of Reno. Burning Man draws more than 60,000 participants from around the world. "Burners" step out of "the default world" and into a community committed to art, creativity, and expression. The Burning Man ethos values radical inclusion and decommodification and runs on a gift economy. The best way to describe the experience might be as magical/radical.

"Yes! I should definitely meet you at Burning Man. But it might be hard to find a ticket just four weeks out." My response to Jennifer's invitation was irrational. And spontaneous. And intuitive.

For years, I'd held out a vague hope that I would one day find my way to Black Rock City to see this grand desert experiment for myself. But the stars had never been close to aligning in favor of the logistically complex, expensive, and time-intensive adventure that is Burning Man.

Recognizing my willingness to cast a line into the water, Jennifer followed my lead, "Okay, well, look. I'll check to see if I can find you a spot in our camp. And you go see if you can find a ticket. If it's meant to be, seems like you'll know pretty quickly."

"Jennifer," I said, "we have a saying here in Texas: 'I ain't scared. Hold my beer.'" Within 10 hours and with very little effort, I had a Burning Man ticket in my hand and a reserved campsite for the week.

With Jennifer's logistical and planning assistance, I had the bike I would need to get around the playa rented, flight booked, and groceries to take along all planned within the week.

It's worth noting that if I had encountered difficulty in finding a ticket or felt that I was "pushing" to make this trip happen, I would have quickly and effortlessly released the idea. I have come to understand and appreciate the importance of being in a healthy easy flow with intuitive impulses like this. And while I wish I could say I'd learned that lesson painlessly, at this point I believe I have finally (mostly) internalized it.

So I came to make my pilgrimage to Black Rock City in August of 2017. At the time, I wasn't completely sure why I said, "Yes" to the Burning Man invitation or why the timing and details worked out so easily.

From the beginning, I had the sense that the trip was related to more than just the shifting winds in my professional life; it also felt somehow related to the sadness and grief I'd been processing about my recent divorce and the loss of my closest cousin to cancer.

At any rate, my curiosity was piqued. I had heard bits and pieces about Burning Man over the years. I'd heard it described as a week-long rave fueled by psychedelics and EDM (Electronic Dance Music), a naked hippy haven with lots of yoga and chakra readings, a countercultural "social experiment" with an economy based on gifting, and a desert-based exhibition of enormous works of art. Still nothing I'd heard prepared me for the sheer other-worldliness of it.

Nearly immediately upon my arrival, I became almost completely helpless. The tremendous desert heat brought me to my knees with searing migraines. For nearly three days, Jennifer and others took loving care of me, bringing me cold compresses, fluids, salt, electrolytes, pain relievers, and a variety of holistic treatments.

Though I'd felt a strong sisterhood with Jennifer from our virtual conversations over Skype and social media, this was my first opportunity to meet her in person. We'd connected seven years earlier through a mutual connection to the School of Lost Borders, the nonprofit organization that conducts the desert-based Vision Fast programs we'd all experienced.

I have always taken a certain amount of pride in my independence and self-sufficiency, so this kind of introduction was for me immensely uncomfortable and humbling. When I tearfully shared these feelings with Jennifer, she just smiled compassionately and said, "We all take care of each other here. It's part of the deal."

Later, she added, "This is just a part of your story. You know Burning Man is a big ceremony, right?"

I didn't really, but as the week progressed I began to understand what she meant.

On one of my orienting bike rides, Jennifer showed me the Temple of Burning Man. I'd heard people talking about the Temple as a large-scale art structure where Burners would come to leave notes memorializing loved ones and to grieve relationships lost. But I had no idea it was such a central feature of Burning Man. The temple is an enormous art construction; I mean, it's an actual temple, and its intricate design incorporates altars, sitting spaces, and interior and exterior gathering areas. Artists and architects submit proposals for the honor of designing and building the temple each year, and it takes a tremendous amount of planning and about 300 skilled volunteers to construct it. I had imagined something much smaller and more on the periphery.

When I entered the temple, I felt my blood rush to my face and my heart pulsing in my ears. My eyes were first drawn to certain large art installations erected in the interior and hung on its walls. These memorials had clearly been designed and constructed by Burners in the months or weeks ahead of Burning Man—then they'd been deconstructed, packed up, and lovingly installed inside the temple. Many of the memorials incorporated large photos, memorabilia, and inscriptions of messages and drawings from friends.

The love and devotion of the makers had been made manifest in these memorials—their immense grief and losses literally laid bare. Scribbled on every plank and erected in every corner was the material expression of the immense beauty of human love and longing, the truest of emotional truths. In this way, that temple delivered me to the most overwhelmingly present human experience I have ever known: this was the divine union of the sacred feminine and the sacred masculine.

Throughout the week, I returned to the temple over and over, sensing the fullness of its expression, sitting with its truth, weeping in its significance, and holding to my chest the treasure of its teachings.

There was a way in which the structure held space for all who knew of it, whether or not we crossed its threshold. There was a way in which the temple connected my griefs and losses to the griefs and losses of all…and then, of course, also connected me to all humans who have themselves ever grieved and lost.

I took my time. I felt my feelings and I wrote my tributes, my memories, and my gratitude to my beloveds lost. I honored them deeply and thanked them for ways they grew, taught, and enriched me. I searched and found the right placement for each of these sacred devotions. Then I wept my losses into that loving dust and left them there.

By the fourth day, I'd finally figured out how to manage my heat sensitivity. I would do most of my exploring during the early morning and evening hours, and I would spend the hottest parts of the day under the camp shade structures, eating pickles, drinking iced coffee, and soaking my feet in ice water.

The bonus of this approach was that it gave me opportunities to visit with other members of our camp as they came in and out of the shade for breaks during the day. I was curious to hear their stories and fascinated that so many of them returned to Burning Man every year. By now, I understood they weren't coming for a breezy good time; this experience was physically challenging and sensorily and emotionally intense. There are much easier ways to have fun and party if that's the intent.

So I asked them lots of questions. I asked about their backgrounds and what their lives were like in the "default world." There were people from the tech and service industries and from the public sector. And there were artists and dancers and acrobats. There were multiple generations represented and a range of takes on sexual orientation and gender expression. I found no consistency in their histories, education, or work experiences.

However, when I asked what prompted them to return every year, I did get a consistent response. Almost to a person, their answers included some variation of the phrase, "I can be fully myself here."

I always followed that answer with additional questions to understand more clearly what they meant. Their responses seemed mostly to point to a freedom they felt in this context to express openly their most creative, loving, emotional aspects. I observed as they embraced and relaxed into the relief of this freedom over the course of the week. Men told their stories of failure and lessons learned, they cried together, and they held each other without reserve or shame.

Many in the camp spoke openly of their deep love and appreciation for the presence and work of others, without it being sexualized, shamed, or misunderstood. They stayed present through conflict, shared their vulnerabilities, held compassionate space for emotional expression, and nurtured each other through physical and emotional challenges. They danced and sang without boundaries or self-consciousness, they created art in and for the moment, and—always—they were met and held in their fullest expressions.

In other words, Burning Man is a context in which the free expression of the feminine-receptive is welcomed along with the masculine-assertive.

Before I arrived, I understood that the week of Burning Man culminated on Saturday with the spectacular burning of an enormous effigy of "the man." There are fire performers and acrobats and laughter and whoops and hollers. The burn is followed by the grandest Dionysian release and celebration which, for many, continues through the following sunrise. My read on this metaphor is that it calls forth ceremonially the intention of liberation from the unbalanced masculine-assertive systems that are psychically and physically burning us out.

I wasn't, however, aware that there was another ceremony at Burning Man. On Sunday, the night before the camps break down and everyone prepares to return to the "default world," they gather one last time to burn the Temple. As this gorgeous structure goes up in flames, so do all the tributes, memorials, and emotions it holds. A departure from the festivities of the previous evening, this gathering is an expression of tremendous reverence. It is a ceremony of communion and release. People hold hands and weep openly; some call out names or make audible tributes to those they've lost; others pray according to a variety of traditions and no tradition. We all said goodbye together.

What if it weren't necessary to camp for a week in 112 degree temperatures to be granted the permission to be fully expressed? If 60,000 people can choose to create such freedom for each other for a week in the desert, we can certainly choose to do the same with at least a few brave and spirited beloveds in our hometowns.

Co-Creation in Barcelona

Two days into a symposium, I found myself standing in front of a kind of collaborative sculpture that seemed to have slowly emerged of its own accord in the center of the room.

The purpose of the gathering was to bring people together to collaborate on solutions to 13 of "the most important issues facing the planet...ranging from educational and financial models to sustainable energy solutions and agriculture."

The Holistic Visions symposium was organized by a UK-based nonprofit under the spiritual guidance of 12 indigenous elders. As I understand it, one of the elders had, while in a meditative state, assigned each participant to a team with a designated area of focus.

When I submitted my name for consideration to participate in the symposium, I assumed, if selected, I would be put to work collaborating on new models for Financial Systems or Seeding Global Community. Instead, I found I'd been assigned to a topic called "Love and Righteousness." I went immediately to the website to read the summary: "Breaking free from systemic dependencies, building up a sense of true love, responsibility, and integrity in order to navigate life purposefully."

I found this description confusing. What did they mean by "systemic dependencies?" How does one define "true love?" How could people ever come to agree on a definition of "righteousness?"

In the weeks leading up to the symposium, our global group of 12 introduced ourselves and began to engage with the topic in the Slack online collaboration channel. As expected, the topic was a slippery one. Aware of our differences in age, culture, and native language, we moved forward slowly and carefully in this online forum. Rather than discussing solutions, most of our interactions focused on coming to a shared understanding of the topic itself.

The old me would have wanted to lead this group. I would have angled to be the "writer of all the things." I would have advocated strongly and rationally for my favorite ideas.

Instead, I decided to use this opportunity to bring what I have learned about the feminine-receptive to engage differently. I wanted to experiment with co-creation. I would bring my most open mind and most receptive mode of being to bear on all interactions in this group. I would refrain from posting my thoughts immediately, allowing my ideas to be informed and enriched by those shared by the others before contributing them for consideration. I would pay close attention to the group's energy, noticing the ideas that bring excitement and inspiration to the group and releasing the ones that do not.

I would step forward to lead a discussion only when I knew with certainty that my experience and wisdom were necessary and supportive. In every other case, I would follow. I would allow silence to be the teacher that it is and would not rush to fill it. I would remain curious and flexible relating to any idea that seemed like "the answer" to allow for it to develop or transform with additional input. I would hear resistance as an opportunity for improvement. Besides finding the approach energizing and exciting, I found it to be much more fun than my old ways of "collaborating."

I enjoyed the mystery of not knowing the answers. It was fascinating to watch how ideas moved through the group. Some ideas emerged, sparked engagement, developed, and advanced. Other ideas, that for me seemed just as promising, failed to inspire, quickly atrophied, and fell away. It was a powerful experience to feel the tension and pull of my old patterns while observing myself not repeating them.

While the online format felt awkward and constricting at times, I found myself enjoying both the people in the group and the opportunity to grapple with such a significant subject. I had never given much consideration to the challenge presented by the fact that there is no shared understanding of the word, "love."

People speak of love in so many different contexts, all with different meanings; we may speak of our love for a good meal, a partner, a child, a sport, and the divine in a single conversation. The greatest poets in history have spent lifetimes and alphabets running this verbal gauntlet. I'm not going to lie; the phrase, "Who do you think you are?" did find its way into my consciousness more than a few times.

Remarkably, we did eventually come to agreement on working definitions of love and righteousness. Love, we decided could be defined "as both a feeling and a unified energetic field, or vibration, of 'oneness.'" This field of love becomes available to us in certain moments when our sense of separation dissolves, "when the barriers of fear, identity, and hurt—individual, cultural, and generational—are dropped." Our definition extended into the implications of such an experience: "This field of love serves to remind us that, while we are having an individual experience in these human bodies with their edges and their mortality, the ultimate enduring truth is that we are not separate."

Aligning on a definition of love provided our group, in turn, a basis for defining "righteousness." If we could define love as the experience of an energetic field of oneness, righteousness could then be defined as the kinds of action we would take if we were aware of our oneness.

Righteousness, then, is what we do and how we conduct ourselves when we know we are not truly separate from others. This definition of righteousness invites us to consider more deeply the universal teaching of the Golden Rule. "Do unto others as you would have them do unto you" can also be understood to mean, "Do unto others knowing that you are simultaneously doing the same unto yourself."

Two months later, when we would first meet each other face-to-face at the symposium, our group used these definitions of Love and Righteousness as a starting place, a foundation for our work together. A diverse mix of people and personalities, we were comprised of healers, artists, community builders, mothers, meditators, business owners, corporate wonks, vegetarians, archers, cooks, joggers, introverts, and over-sharers who'd converged on Barcelona from all over the world.

It wasn't long before things began to get trippy. Each day in the morning plenary session, the symposium groups were all assembled and given a set of instructions and objectives for the day's work together. And each day, just after the plenary session, it became clear that those instructions and objectives didn't remotely apply to us or the work we were called to do as a group focused on Love and Righteousness. Our mission, again, was to propose innovative solutions or projects that would support the planet in "breaking free from systemic dependencies, building up a sense of true love, responsibility, and integrity in order to navigate life purposefully." There was a collective concern within our group about the pressure of "project plans" or "milestones." We knew we needed to approach this work differently, to use different approaches than the ones that evolved from the existing systems and models. Our work together would not be predictable. It would not be linear. It wouldn't be pushed, thought, or scheduled into being. The work we did together was creative. It was inspired and alive. It spiraled itself into emergence because our group cultivated the conditions for it. We breathed it in, allowed it to guide us, moved with it, and ultimately became it.

At one point, a group member was leading us through a structured whiteboard activity to imagine and capture a framework, describing the conditions under which new systems or organizations based on a love vibration might be created.

With that activity still in process, another group member spontaneously went to the opposite white board, picked up a marker, and began drawing trees, then roots, then a network of fine lines connecting the tree roots to each other, then mushrooms. After a few minutes, the group turned its attention away from the words and toward the tree diagram.

"The Mother Trees," the artist explained, "come first." She went on, "Mother Trees put down their roots and create the initial conditions by which the mushrooms and the connective network of mycelium fungus can germinate and grow. And the beautiful thing then is that this connective network creates a community out of the trees, establishing a way for them to communicate with each other. In this way, an entire forest can know itself!"

It was quite a beautiful rendering and seemed at first unrelated to the initial discussion. The group sat still momentarily, uncertain of how to proceed. Then someone asked, pointing back to the text and Post-it notes on the other whiteboard, "Okay, if we look at the framework we are describing over here…and if we want to

cultivate the conditions for new systems based on love and connectedness...what would the Mother Trees be in this model?"

This question and connection immediately energized the
group, giving us a nature-based metaphor to use as a guide and
foundation for imagining ways to support the emergence of new
love-based systems. Who would the Mother Trees be in a human
system that has as its basis a knowing of love and oneness? New
ideas spun up from this question informing our framework.

This is how our work together went. Art became an integral
part of the process. Or maybe the process itself became art.

So here I was...staring at the sculpture, trancelike. "The water
is there...the people...the broken pieces...and there...the elders...
hang on...." There was more that I can't remember. The individual
voices around me hummed and mixed together in my mind.

I no longer recognized who was saying what or even if my own
voice was among them. And then, after a few seconds of silence, a
sudden simultaneous realization and exclamation, "It's upside down!"

We all knew it to be true and two or three among us went
immediately to work putting it right. The room buzzed as they
quickly removed from the ad hoc art piece the broken pottery, the
flickering candle, and the water feature. As they flipped over the
central element of the sculpture, a heavy wire stool that had been
pilfered from the foyer on the second day, I felt a spontaneous
laugh wash over me. The flat surface of the stool seat was now on
the ground, leaving the top of the sculpture open. Even before all
the other components of the composition were replaced, it was
clear this reversal was correct. There was an undeniable shift, a
kind of release or opening in the energetic flow of the room.

In a different context, at any previous time in my life, this
experience would have left me speechless. But, by the third day,

when we flipped this sculpture over, I had come to expect the extraordinary in our group dynamics.

Two days earlier, on the first day of the symposium, our group had dropped into a deep co-creative space unlike anything I had ever experienced.

We began that day and each of the two following days with a shared meditation and a round of council practice. Council practice is the deep group communication practice that I had originally been taught at Naropa. The second day we added synchronized breathing.

So, as a group, we opened our time together with a shared experience of the feminine-receptive, practicing collective inspiration and deep listening before beginning—before even deciding on—our work together. There were times when it felt as if we were moving as a oneness, creating as a single body.

By the second day, our group was spiraling together more naturally, moving from our topic intention, to our definitions, to our Post-it framework, to our mycelium diagram, to a poem that had come to one of us in the middle of the night, to creative sharing in our council circle, and back around again with new insights.

I had been standing at the whiteboard considering our working description of the framework when the wire stool sculpture began to emerge. Hearing activity behind me, I turned around to see four of our group members busily at work in the center of the room. There was no one giving instructions. Someone had apparently initiated it by bringing the stool in from the foyer—I didn't see who. One member of the group said it needed water and, filling a bowl began to experiment with different ways of incorporating it. Another was cutting a people chain out of a brown paper bag left over from the morning's breakfast. Someone else left on a mission and quickly returned with a plant, placing it on top as if nothing could be more obvious. Another lit and incorporated a candle. No one seemed to be in charge, and no one seemed to know the end-state.

When this creative energy had run its course and the sculpture seemed complete, we gathered around it, examining its features with curiosity. Someone asked what it meant. A couple of possibilities emerged from the group, but no one claimed to know the answer.

Our assignment for that day had been to create a showcase of our proposals to share in a poster session with the other symposium groups. We'd been instructed to summarize our work and plans to date on a poster and hang it on the wall outside our group's break-out room to be viewed and discussed with the symposium facilitators and attendees as they walked around.

At that point, we had not progressed our framework, so we decided to hang up our definitions of Love and Righteousness along with a sketch of a heart with roots. A couple of our group members felt inspired to display the mysterious sculpture as well, sensing it would be useful to ask the other symposium attendees to share what they saw in it. Remarkably, their collective responses seemed to indicate that the sculpture was both a model of the symposium itself—incorporating the elders and the land and the water and the inspiration and the connectedness of its participants—and also of the world, with its elders and its land and its inspiration and the connectedness of all.

So, on the third day, once the art piece had been deconstructed and reconstructed in reverse, our group paused to take it in. We marveled at the details. The paper people chain that spiraled around the sculpture's exterior had mostly remained in place, but the reversal made the people in the chain appear to be more active, as if they were reaching for and helping each other. With the top of the sculpture now open, the supporting elements were now all grounded, the candle's reflection flickering on the surface of the water.

Then slowly, we each found our way to what was next. Two or three drifted over to the whiteboard to once again take in the previous day's drawing of the forest with its Mother Trees, mushrooms, and connective mycelium network. A few returned to the whiteboard with its collection of words, lines, Post-it notes, and circles. Others took a quick break to grab a coffee or step outside.

Our time together at the symposium was coming to an end, and we'd been asked to prepare and deliver a final presentation summarizing the outcomes of our work together. By then, we'd made some good progress on our Love and Righteousness Framework, but we knew it wasn't near ready for primetime. Per the instructions delivered to us during the morning full-group session, each team would have five minutes to present a summary of their solutions—along with proposed projects and high-level plans—to the final assembly of symposium contributors and organizers.

Earlier in the day, our group had been agitated, expressing concern about the final presentation and feeling the need to scramble and complete the very sketchy draft of our framework. While we knew the work couldn't be rushed, we felt a strong responsibility to represent our effort well.

As the time drew near, a sense of ease seemed to descend upon our group. I can't speak for what others felt, but I knew that what we had accomplished was somehow substantial, perhaps even momentous. Even though we had not completed something that our existing cultural and organizational paradigms would validate as "successful," there was something important that transpired as a result of our willingness to move together differently.

Our group dynamic had released something, had set some energy in motion that—through some universal truth, butterfly effect, or quantum physics—was spiraling its way through the collective, possibly generating more of the very co-creative energy we'd been trying to describe in our framework. I sensed in it a balance of feminine-receptive and masculine-assertive energies the likes of which I had never before experienced in a group. The feminine-receptive allowed us to integrate the various gifts and insights from the group, so we were able to engage the masculine-assertive aspects to develop plans and actions.

With 15 minutes to go, we agreed to share some of our inspirations along with a few of the elements of our framework. I felt our collective energy swirling as we sat together in the final plenary.

When we were called, we held hands and faced the audience, hearts open. The air thick with feeling, one of our group members read the poem that had provided inspiration for our work together. I spoke next, sharing our definitions of Love and Righteousness from the center of my heart and from my deepest knowing. Others in the group shared certain elements of the framework that they felt most strongly connected to. Tears came for a few of us, and a reverent hush fell over the entire group. There were no questions from the facilitators.

CHAPTER 10

My Quest Continues

It's been over 20 years since my mind was blown by Dawn, the San Francisco psychic.

Now at age 55, I feel more alive and vibrant than ever, and my journey continues to illuminate ways for me to deepen, expand, and balance my expression. Perhaps in part because this effort has been so intentional for me, I see clearly and appreciate the contrast between the 31-year-old young woman walking back to her hotel in San Francisco and the person I am now, sitting at the computer writing these words.

We have a lot in common, that young woman and me. I have her intense curiosity and willingness to risk being wrong, over and over again. I share her appreciation for the big picture, clear instructions, clean floors, and obscure facts about famous people. I still benefit daily from her willingness to work hard in the world and to focus more on possibilities than limitations. And I still love hard and hold tight to my family and friends.

All of the aspects of who I was then continue to inhabit, in-form, and occasionally plague me. What's different for me today is that I have come to know and express myself more fully and with more flexibility. I continue to awaken to my emotional life and to allow its expression to teach and activate me, even when what it has to teach me is painful.

And these lessons open me to ever increasing depths of my own gentleness, compassion, and receptivity. It is from that deep, expansive place that I find myself more and more able to sense what is needed and to bring comfort and nurturing to myself and others.

Today, I more readily recognize and honor the knowings that come to me in nonlinear, nonrational ways. Remaining open to the flashing wisdom of my intuition keeps my life unfolding in ever more interesting and inspiring trajectories than any I could have devised or planned for logically.

Over the years, as I have become more capable of expressing my feminine-receptive, I have become more practiced at maintaining a healthy balance between my feminine and masculine expres-sions. And I sense this within my being as a powerful sort of al-chemical spark; it's engaged me in a thrilling process of co-creation of inner and outer, of seen and unseen, of individual and infinite, of spirit and material. The writing of this book represents my most ambitious experiment of this co-creative process to date…and I can already feel the next one lining up behind it.

Perfect and imperfect, my story continues to be written.

I invite you to come around in the spiral with me, to reawaken, remember, and celebrate the divine receptive feminine within you and to balance it with the inspired active masculine. I invite you to notice and join the spiral of awakenings in your communities as a basis for co-creating new systems, systems that reflect our recognition that the collective good can never be in conflict with the individual good...because truly we are both.

I extend to you the blessings of my grandmothers and my grandfathers, ever with me.

The End

Acknowledgements

I owe a tremendous debt of gratitude to those whose writings and teachings on the archetypal and divine feminine and masculine have inspired and informed this book, including Carl Jung, Marion Woodman, and Joanna Macy as well as indigenous and native peoples from all places down through time.

I am ever grateful to my parents, Robert Gates, Ellie Ashley, and LeVern Ashley, for their unconditional love and unwavering support and to my maternal and paternal grandparents and my ancestors, now on the other side, for the legacy of their lessons learned, debts paid, and gifts passed down. In particular, I thank my grandmother/godmother, Christina Tambourides, whose spirit often joins me in my daily prayers and meditations. I thank my brother, cousins, and my entire extended family whose love, affection, and humor have buoyed me through the most difficult times of my life. I acknowledge my cousin, Jenny "Hane" Nicolaou Newlin, now departed this life, for sharing the gifts of her wonder and curiosity with me and for the love I continue to feel from her spirit, ever present.

For their friendship and the abundance of encouragement, assistance, and love they've extended to me throughout this often bumpy creative process, I extend my thanks to Ann Al-Bahish, Jessica Eason, Nanine Ewing, Debbie Giroux, Jennifer Giroux, Michael Gott, Tina Hart, Jen Houston, Shelly Immel, Tom Stell, Hari Kirn Khalsa, Sat Kartar Khalsa, Gary Lachance, Jen Lemen, Susan P. Parker, Suzanne Quentin, Max Regan, Maya Stein, Amy Tingle, Tami Ren, and the warrior women of the circle—Sara Eliason, Brielle Rouse, and Becky Restum.

I am deeply thankful to William Berger, Shannon Hart, Kimberley Cambron, Jesse Berger, Nate Hart, Marin Hart, Haley Cambron, and Grant Cambron for all they have taught me and continue to teach me about grace, love, balance, and forgiveness. They are forever family, beloved and held with tremendous tenderness in my heart.

Finally, I thank my partner in love and life, Stephanie Briggs, for taking in my story so completely and for inspiring me in every moment to live more bravely into the desires of my heart.

Attributes of Balanced Expression
(Reference Table)

ATTRIBUTES OF BALANCED EXPRESSION

Masculine-Assertive *Yang / Animus*	+	Feminine-Receptive *Yin / Anima*
speaking		listening
doing		being
planned		spontaneous
thinking / intellectual		feeling / emotional
individual		communal
logical		intuitive
deductive / linear		integrative / cyclical
active		still
directive		nurturing
separate		unified
competitive		cooperative
exhale		inhale
structure		flow

CPSIA information can be obtained
at www.ICGtesting.com
Printed in the USA
BVHW081913220321
603177BV00006B/325